What
Your Boss
NEVER
Told You

The Quick Start
Guide for New Managers

Gary Winters

What Readers Are Saying About
What Your Boss Never Told You

In the same way that we aren't given a human operating manual to make sense of life, or a parenting manual at the birth of our kids, in our careers most of us are not blessed with a manager's quick start manual as we transition to a leadership role.

Gary Winters, in *What Your Boss Never Told You*, bridges this knowledge and experience gap with poignant anecdotes, razor sharp insights and actionable ways to jump start your career as well as that of your team, when leadership and management become mission critical. It includes just about everything you wanted to know but didn't know how to ask with respect to getting started in management and includes some timeless gems for the seasoned manager as well.

I wish somebody had shared these insights with me early in my career! This will be required reading for those I have the privilege and responsibility to mentor on the road ahead.

Neville Billimoria
Senior Vice President & Chief Advocacy Officer
Mission Federal Credit Union
San Diego CA

Where was this book those many years ago at the start of my career? It would surely have eased some of the hard knocks I have had to endure. I am glad I found it and I especially loved the 2+2=4 example in Chapter Six. Gary Winters + *What Your Boss Never Told You* = a successful manager!

Craig D. Bronzan
Director of Parks and Recreation
Brentwood, CA

Gary Winters is the Yoda of management consultants! Reading *What Your Boss Never Told You* is like having a wise, experienced, and articulate guide by your side - offering you powerful, practical advice.

Keep this little book within easy reach - so you can refer to it on a regular basis. The practices and principles he writes about will make you a better leader.

Eric Klein
Principal, Dharma Consulting
San Diego, CA

While reading *What Your Boss Never Told You*, I saw myself on nearly every page. I was either nodding my head in agreement or letting out a low hum as I thought, "I wish had thought of that when I had to supervise people." This book will undoubtedly help new supervisors and managers, who as is so rightly point out, are never told the full length, width, and depth of their new positions.

Let me add this is a book all managers and supervisors should read, whether they are new on the job or not.

I believe that a person should leave at least three things as a legacy. One is a box of personal journals, the second is a gallery of photographs, and the third is a library of books. I want *What Your Boss Never Told You* to be part of my library when my descendants review the things that have had an influence on me.

David Royall
Retired Air Traffic Control Manager
Palm City, Florida

What a wonderful tool for any new manager, or any manager humble enough to admit that they might be rusty in a few areas! *What Your Boss Never Told You* is a quick and often humorous read that offers foundational tips and how-to's to succeed as a manager at any level.

June Dudas
Assistant Director
City of Poway, CA

Gary provides wisdom in short, easy-to-digest bites. This is a must-read for all new managers or anyone considering taking on a management role.

Susan Gerke
Gerke Consulting and Development
Laguna Nigel, CA

What Your Boss Never Told You is an excellent, concise book for new and not-so-new managers. I enjoyed reading the principles about "flowing up," "flowing down," and letting the team figure out how to do the work. There is a key section on moral values and leadership – good to see someone emphasize that openly.

The most important section of the book for me was the chapter on consensus. It improves my leadership skills by understanding better what consensus really involves. I recommend Gary's book to those who appreciate acquiring new knowledge from a pro.

Donald W. Larson
San Marcos, CA

What Your Boss NEVER Told You

The Quick Start Guide For New Managers

Gary Winters

San Diego, California

Author Online!

For updates and more resources, visit Gary Winters' webpage and *Leadership Almanac* blog at

www.garywinters.com

To Dianne

Without whose love, support, advice and patience
this book would not exist.

About the Author

Gary Winters has worked with scores of leaders over the past 25 years in all kinds of organizations – large, small, in both the public sector and private sector. Based in San Diego but available nation-wide, his services include:

- One on one coaching
- Team building
- Leadership workshops and academies – design and delivery
- Keynote speaking

Gary created *The Leadership Almanac* in 2008, a blog where you can find dozens of articles with practical wisdom about the art of leadership.

He is the co-author (with Eric Klein) of *To Do or Not To Do: How Successful Leaders Make Better Decisions.*

Contact Information:

Web: www.garywinters.com

Email: gary@garywinters.com

Phone: 619-840-0148

Contents

Foreword

I first met Gary Winters over twenty-five years ago, while serving as the leader of an internal Organization Development unit. He'd been asked to create and deliver a new Supervisors Academy for us, and he did it splendidly.

Throughout my career, it's been a special gift to meet practitioners who were both clear and creative. This is not to be taken for granted – so when I see it, I take heed. That's why I found myself paying close attention to Gary's work.

Reading *What Your Boss Never Told You* reminds me of those early days, watching Gary in action before audiences of eager supervisors.

Leadership Development programs are designed to share the latest thinking about systems and strategy, employee motivation, performance reviews, and the like. But if truth be told, participants are also hungry for specific and practical solutions to the problems they face every day.

As one example: I remember watching as a participant said, "I need help! What should I do with a subordinate who comes to me to solve a problem when he has the ability to solve it himself?"

Gary has always been on the mark when he responds to questions like these during his workshops. In this instance, he quickly dashed to the chart stand and began to diagram the downside of what some have called "learned helplessness," and then he offered several practical suggestions that were quickly understood.

A gifted storyteller, he has a knack for sharing a yarn to illustrate a learning point. He might describe a famous historical event, for example, to pinpoint the serious implications for a manager making a decision without appropriate input from staff.

His previous book, *To Do or Not To Do – How Successful Leaders Make Better Decisions*, written with Eric Klein, is filled with anecdotes that are not quickly forgotten. And Gary freely shares the mistakes he made during his own management career to help others avoid them.

When I read *What Your Boss Never Told What You*, I was impressed with how much practical advice lies between its covers. It's as though the reader is sitting in one of Gary's workshops, getting one sound suggestion after another.

I've seen how the participants in his workshops eat this up. I know – because they've told me – how grateful they were that the "secret in the sauce" wasn't held back from them, or left for them to figure out themselves. Now, what

Gary has shared with thousands of participants in person is available to everyone who reads this book.

He bills the book as a "Quick Start Guide" for newly promoted managers, but make no mistake – there's something in here for everyone, from the newcomer to the seasoned manager. There's gold on these pages for anyone in a leadership position.

We need more books like this in the field of Organization Development. Books written by someone who has been there and done that. Someone who has made mistakes, had successes, and really knows that works and what doesn't. This is applied work at its best and it is work that makes me proud of our profession.

If the goal of Organization Development practitioners is to make the workplace better, and to strengthen the thinking and capacity of leaders and their organizations in the process, then Gary has hit the mark. *What Your Boss Never Told You* does just that.

I've been in the field for thirty-two years and I've been around the block a bit when it comes to observing management consultants and OD practitioners. I see who really helps people instead of confusing them, who is genuinely experienced enough to provide tools that really work, who people listen to, and who can actually move a manager to take a new action. Gary Winters has clearly – and creatively – demonstrated these abilities in his new book.

Trust me, it is a read that will be helpful to anyone in a leadership position. Keep *What Your Boss Never Told You* on your shelf at work. You will be referring to it many times.

Trudy J. Sopp, Ph.D.
Founder & Consulting Partner,
THE CENTRE For Organization Effectiveness
La Jolla, California

Introduction

Recently, I purchased a sophisticated digital camera with more features than I could have imagined. It has the latest technology to produce breathtaking images – *if* you know how it works. Of course, I can put it into an automatic mode and get some good pictures without ever learning how to take advantage of this technology. But if all I wanted was some acceptable snaps, I would have purchased a simple "point and shoot" camera. I bought this model because I want a higher quality result – I'm a committed amateur photographer.

I'm also impatient.

I wanted to get started right away learning to operate my new camera. Fortunately, it came with two guides to do so – a Quick Start guide, and a longer, highly detailed Owner's Manual.

When I first became a manager many years ago, I felt the same way about my new job as I feel about my camera. I wanted great results – as soon as possible. I wish I'd had some kind of Quick Start guide back then and a comprehensive "Owner's Manual" for new managers. I would have read the Quick Start guide quickly to get an initial grasp of my new job, and been able to hit the ground running. There is no doubt in my mind I would have avoided many of the mistakes I made during my transition from being an individual contributor to being a manager.

But there was no Quick Start guide.

Plus, the closest things to an Owner's Manual were the books I found on management practice – which were often overwhelming, intimidating, or just too academic to be of much use at that early stage of my career.

I'm the first to tell you that the Owner's Manual for my camera cannot be faulted for being incomplete. Between its covers it describes each of the hundreds of features on the camera. If I want to change the f-stop, adjust the shutter speed, or reset the white balance, I can look in the manual to learn how to do that. But it is *still* overwhelming and intimidating!

And there is one critical shortcoming – the Owner's Manual doesn't tell me *why* I might want to do those things.

WELCOME TO THE QUICK START GUIDE

What Your Boss Never Told You is for you if you've recently been promoted to a management position or you're thinking about becoming a manager, and you want to hit the ground running. It doesn't attempt to cover everything there is to know about being an effective manager. It doesn't drill deeply into common management practices such as conducting interviews or setting goals or monitoring performance.

Instead, in a series of twenty-one brief chapters, this book gives you *ways to think about* being a manager – how to frame the challenges and rewards of leading people.

If you're lucky, you attended a *Making Your Transition into Management* workshop shortly before or after you accepted the position to explore your new assignment.

But, if you're typical, this didn't happen. You were given the job, met the people you were about to supervise (if you don't know them already), filled out some paperwork, and given a start date. The rest, as they say, was up to you.

What Your Boss Never Told You is a collection of important ideas about what it means to be a manager in today's organizations, some basic and relevant principles of human behavior, and information about what highly effective managers do in contrast with their peers.

The title of this book is clearly a hook, designed to get you to crack the cover and explore the insides. But let's face it – *How to Be a Good Manager* isn't that sexy. It doesn't sell. And if it doesn't sell, then good people like you never get the benefits of what's inside.

So is this book really about things your boss never told you? I believe so.

There are some great bosses out there who excel at mentoring others – but there are far more who don't. And even if you work for a Great Boss, and hope to emulate him or her in your own leadership practice, the odds are still pretty good that your boss hasn't shared all of this information with you – because most bosses haven't spent the time organizing it in this way. For example:

· Has your boss told you about the three kinds of employees you will be managing and the implications of this for your management practice?

- Has your boss ever talked about the best two-word job description of an effective manager?
- Has your boss passed on to you what most people really want from their boss?
- Have you discussed how and when to include your staff in your decision-making process?

I'm betting not.

I'M NOT KNOCKING YOUR BOSS!

Most managers aren't as skilled (or committed) as we might like them to be in developing new managers. And let's face it – most of them weren't carefully and consciously coached themselves when they took their first management position. Add to that they have many priorities – and getting you "coached up" is but one of them.

Perhaps "Lesson #1" should be this: *your development as a manager is really up to you.* You must make the commitment to some honest self-assessment and find the resources to develop your skills. This book is a great place to start.

A LITTLE ABOUT ME

So who am I to be writing a Quick Start Guide?

I'm a leadership coach and workshop facilitator with over twenty-five years experience working with leaders in small and large organizations, in both the public and private sector.

I run a successful blog, *The Leadership Almanac*, (the link is www.garywinters.com) which has a simple but powerful mission: to describe what successful leaders do so that others can do these things as well. To date, thousands of people have visited and taken away valuable insights.

My passion, throughout my career, has been to find out how great managers "tick," and teach that to others. I have worked with thousands of managers, consulted to over 200 organizations, and spent the time to refine what I've learned about effective management so I could pass it along to others.

I've also been a full-time manager, with all the joys and headaches that come with the job. I made the transition from "individual contributor" to manager myself - and made many mistakes along the way. I wrote this book to facilitate a much more successful transition for you.

The ideas in this book have been presented in countless workshops and I use them when I coach individual leaders. All of them are "field tested" and found to have value. By the way, all of the people you'll meet in the book are real people. I've used only their first names to preserve their anonymity.

What Your Boss Never Told You is organized into twenty-one chapters. They can be read in any order. Some build on others (and I've pointed that out so you'll know what goes with what). Most are complete by themselves. I like to keep things "bite-sized," so you can read just one in just a few minutes. It's a habit I've learned from running my blog, *The Leadership Almanac* – keep things simple.

Some readers may choose to read one chapter a day for three weeks. Others will "pick and choose" something to read every now and then. Some will read the whole darn book in one setting – perhaps on their Kindle or iPad on an airplane headed to a conference.

IT'S ALL GOOD

Start with something that catches your eye. I encourage you to jot down your thoughts and reactions in a notebook as you read and make this a more interactive experience. It will help anchor the content in your head, and increase the probability that you will start using these ideas immediately.

When I wrote this guide, I imagined you and I were sitting in a café, talking and sharing our experiences with one another. Each chapter emerged as a response to a question you might have raised, or a point you might have made, or an issue you were trying to understand.

My hope is that *What Your Boss Never Told You* will be an effective Quick Start guide as you launch your management career. Afterwards, you'll want to deepen your understanding with other books, seminars, and even blogs that explore management practice even further. You'll find recommendations for these resources at the end of the book.

As you take your leadership practice to a higher level and become a more confident, competent manager, you will truly enjoy the rewards and immense personal satisfaction of leading people to do great things.

For people who have chosen a management career, there are few things better than that.

Ready? Let's get started...

Part One: Your Transition

Making the transition from being an individual contributor to a manager can be one of the most challenging periods of your career.

Sadly, many organizations pay scant attention to this transition process. New managers are often put in a "sink or swim" situation. That's should never happen!

In the Quick Start chapters ahead, you will gain insight into what skills will serve you best as a manager, the (often unspoken) questions about you that your staff will have (and how to answer them), five classic transition mistakes you'll want to avoid, and five management habits you don't want to form.

CHAPTER ONE

What Got You to the Party
May Get You Shown to the Door

Have you ever wondered why you were chosen for a leadership role in your organization?

Unless you're the exception, I'd bet you were selected because you have robust technical skills in your field and a track record of achievement. The prevailing belief seems to be that people who are excellent at doing something should be put in charge of others doing the same thing.

Technical skills are the "things you do" as an individual contributor. Most folks believe that if they do well enough at their job, they will eventually be promoted to management (like it or not!). That's how it works in most organizations.

Great marketing professionals become brand managers. Great financial analysts become finance managers. Great sales people become sales managers, and so on.

Odds are that your technical skills set you apart, got you noticed, and earned you this promotion. They got you to the party.

Good for you!

But – what got you to the party may, in time, get you shown to the door. Great technical skills alone do not make for good managers. And over-relying on your technical skills is a huge mistake.

GREAT MANAGERS HAVE AT LEAST THREE SKILL SETS

1. Technical skills

2. Organizational (also called political) skills

3. Interpersonal skills

Here's some plain truth your boss may never have told you: *your technical skills are going to erode the longer you remain in management.* You won't be using them as often, and you're going to get rusty. Advances in your field are going to occur without you using those skills every day. What you must understand is that you're no longer in the "technology business."

You're in the "people business."

Let's drill down.

ORGANIZATIONAL SKILLS

They're called organizational skills in polite company. They're really *political* skills – they allow you to successfully maneuver in your organization. They're about "how to get things done" where you work.

People with good political skills know how things *really* work in their organizations – as opposed to knowing how things are *supposed* to work. They know who really holds power and who doesn't, whose support is critical to introduce a new product, system, or proposal, and how to position their priorities in the best possible light.

They use these skills:

·   To compete with other managers for scarce, finite resources

- To calculate the risk of doing something that they believe trumps established policy or procedure
- To determine when to go to the mat, and when to walk away
- To manage their own boss

INTERPERSONAL SKILLS

You'll need interpersonal skills every time you:

- Coach a team member
- Help resolve a conflict between members of your team
- Deliver performance feedback
- Mentor someone
- Run a meeting

If you're going to succeed as a manager, you must develop strong political and interpersonal skills.

You can see this easily in athletics. Rarely are Hall of Fame caliber players successful as managers or coaches – yet they have "technical skills" in abundance.

Tommy Lasorda, former manager of the Los Angeles Dodgers, played as a major league pitcher for just three seasons, compiling a forgettable win-loss record of 0-4 in 26 games.

But as a manager, he guided his teams to four pennants and two World Series titles, retiring with a record of 1,599 wins against 1,439 losses (a .526 percentage). He understood baseball, and more important, he understood his players. He didn't succeed as a manger because he was a terrific player – he succeeded with superior interpersonal skills.

As an individual contributor, you thrived by solving technical challenges. Now you're expected to solve "people" problems. *If you rely on your technical expertise and neglect the human side of leadership, eventually you will be shown the door.*

Your strengths will have become your liability.

Too harsh?

Perhaps.

If you're one of the fortunate few who brought great people and political skills together with your technical skills to your new position, all the better. But if you're like most folks, you spent years honing your technical skills and became so accomplished that they put you in charge. If you want to succeed as a manager, you must focus on developing your political and interpersonal skills.

CHAPTER TWO

Keep Your Dial Tuned to WIIFM

When you're the new sheriff in town, the first thing people are going to do is ask themselves "What's in it for me?" The question has even become an acronym: WIIFM.

They want to know, as soon as possible, what your new assignment will mean to them. What kind of boss are you going to be? What will be your priorities, your goals, your hot buttons? How easy will it be to work for you? What do you plan to change, and what will remain the same? How well are you regarded in the organization? What's your track record? How much do you understand about what's been going on in the department? The list can seem endless.

No doubt you've already begun thinking about some of these questions and plan to let your team know as soon as possible. An all-hands, "meet the new boss" meeting is pretty standard fare.

The problem is, most of these meetings fall short because they ignore some fundamental questions that will be on their minds – as well as yours.

There is solid research showing that when a new manager takes charge, productivity drops – sometimes dramatically. While people sort out who you are, (and not just in terms of your goals and priorities) their focus on their jobs will lie somewhere south of 100%. Off-line conversations will begin as people compare notes and pass along anecdotes they've heard about you. Don't be shocked. It's natural, it's normal, and you can view it as an opportunity, not a problem.

If you ignore this dynamic, there will be consequences. As the old commercial said, "You can pay me now, or you can pay me later." In terms of productivity, letting people "figure you out" on their own takes much longer and productivity *will* suffer.

This means you have a choice to make right now, at the beginning of your new assignment. You can manage this process, or you can let it unfold by itself.

It's all up to you.

It's not just the big things

Much of what your people want to understand isn't just the "big picture." It's the little things. Your pet peeves. Your work habits. Your ground rules.

Some of these might be things you haven't even thought about. But they are important issues, as people take their measure of you - just as you will be taking your measure of them.

Let's start with ground rules, or what I call the "rules of engagement." These are often unspoken expectations about how things are done within a group of people.

For example, I'd wager that in most staff meetings you've attended each member of the staff always sits in the same chair. Ever wonder why?

Do you suppose the boss called everyone together and made an agreement on which chair belongs to which member of the team? Probably not – the pattern simply evolved with the passage of time, and became obvious, if never even mentioned, to everyone. What makes it a rule of engagement?

The answer is revealed in another question: what happens if someone sits in a different seat? They're likely to be greeted with a mumbled "Excuse me, you're sitting in 'my' seat!" comment from a co-worker. They've "broken" the rule.

We learn most of the ground rules that govern our lives by accident, often by unintentionally breaking them. Early in my career, the way I discovered my boss hated email updates was by doing just that – sending her email updates. She had never thought to mention that she preferred her staff to pop in her office occasionally with a quick oral update.

It didn't occur to her to tell me this, until I "broke" the rule. How was I to know? I couldn't read her mind – and your new staff can't read yours, either. I had to break the rule to learn the rule.

So here you are, the new boss, and suddenly *everything* is called into question. Everyone has to figure things out. While they're busy figuring out the new boss (and comparing notes), they're less productive than they would be otherwise.

Years ago, the United States Navy recognized this problem. The Navy has a long history of changing Commanding Officers (COs) every two years throughout the service. Their studies showed that productivity in a given unit would dip whenever a new CO assumed command, and that productivity didn't return to previous levels for an average of six months.

Six months!

Since the typical CO only had a two year tenure in any given assignment, he or she was faced with less than full productivity one fourth of the time. That was not acceptable.

What the Navy discovered could easily be true for you as well – you might be facing months of less-than-optimal productivity, all because everyone (you and the team) is spending valuable "work" time trying to figure each other out.

The Navy solved this problem with a process called the Transition Workshop, in which the in-coming commander and the team assembled for a carefully designed meeting.

At this meeting, the new commander was given a list of questions by a facilitator, and sent to another room to prepare his or her answers. During that time, the team was also given a similar list of questions, and as a group they worked on their responses.

The commander and the team would reassemble and have a dialogue about the questions and the answers. It was an "everything you wanted to know about each other but didn't know how to ask" session.

YOU CAN REPLICATE THIS PROCESS

You may not have the luxury of having a facilitated off-site retreat to kick-start your own transition, but you can borrow the design from the Navy and facilitate the process yourself.

You'll start with two lists of questions – one for you, and one for your team. I've put together potential questions later in this chapter.

Assemble everyone, and tell them the purpose of the meeting is to get to know one another better on a more personal and practical level, so that the team can stay focused on it's mission.

Next, read the questions you're going to answer, and the questions you'd like them to answer as a group without you in the room. Give them enough time to write their answers while you write yours.

Reassemble the group and have a dialogue, going back and forth from a question for you and a question for the team. Expand your answers as the dialogue unfolds if they have additional questions.

Here are some sample questions you can put on the list for you to answer. There are many more questions for you than for them, and you do not have to use them all – but remember, if you do not talk about something, your team will spend time trying to figure it out.

TRANSITION QUESTIONS FOR YOU:

- How do you describe your job, in words a twelve-year-old would understand?
- What are three or four words that describe you?
- What are three or four words that describe how you'll approach your new job?

- What are some of your hopes for the coming year?
- What concerns do you have about the coming year?
- Why did you accept this assignment? (What's in it for you?)
- As a leader, what are your major strengths as you understand them?
- What aspect(s) of your leadership practice are you hoping to develop further?
- What are some of your core values? How do they play out on the job?
- What do people have to do to earn your trust?
- How will your team know if you think something is very important?
- How will people know if you're dissatisfied?
- How do you prefer to receive critical information?
- How do you go about organizing your time?
- How do you like to make important decisions?
- If you've planted your stake firmly on an issue, and someone wants you to re-address the issue, how should they approach you?
- If someone thinks you're making a mistake, what should they do?
- What are the ground rules about calling you at home or after hours in general?
- What are your pet peeves, if any?
- What are your initial impressions of the team?

QUESTIONS FOR YOUR STAFF:

- What are some things you hope to learn about me?

- What are some words or phrases that best describe our team?

- What are some of the strengths of our team?

- What kinds of things does our team do well?

- What kinds of things does our team not do so well?

- What are some of the hopes our team has for the coming year?

- What are some of the concerns our team has for the coming year?

- What are some of the things we hope to gain with a new manager?

- What are some of our concerns about getting a new manager?

- What are some of the core values of our team?

- What are the highest priorities for the team right now?

- What are some of the unwritten ground rules we've operated on that you (the new manager) should know about?

- What should you know about our decision-making process as a team?

- What words would we use to describe our team meetings?

If you conduct a transition meeting, you will learn much about your team – both from their answers to their questions, and by how they answer them. They will learn much about you as well. Keep it casual, keep it light, but encourage candor. An advantage of a transition meeting is that everyone on your team hears the same message from you at the same time. This keeps rumors to a minimum.

Even with a spectacular transition meeting, you can expect a temporary dip in productivity as the team and you adjust to one another. But the time this takes will be significantly reduced.

This is the best way I know for you to "hit the ground running."

May the Force be with you.

CHAPTER THREE

Five Mistakes to Avoid
When They Put You in Charge

Warning! At some point, it's going to happen – maybe it already has. Your promotion to be the new manager is going to go to your head, which will make it swell, which in turn is will make it harder for you to see things clearly.

It's natural – you're proud of your achievement – as well you should be. You should celebrate, and bask in the glow of your adoring fans (primarily these will be found at home, by the way, or amongst friends who don't work in your organization. Trust me on this one.)

When (notice, I didn't say "if") this happens to you, take heart. You can avoid some of the unfortunate consequences of an overblown sense of self importance.

Here are five classic mistakes that new leaders often make. Once you know them, you can avoid them.

MISTAKE #1: THINKING THIS PROMOTION IS ABOUT YOU, WHEN REALLY IT'S ABOUT THEM

As you begin your new assignment, it's quite tempting to be seduced by the congratulations, the accolades, and all the possibilities. But you must resist the idea that this important event is all about you. It's not, particularly to your new staff. You can bet the farm that what's on each of the minds of the people who now report to you is WIIFM – what's in it for me?

And rightly so, because the truth is, they don't work for you. You work for them. Your new team will succeed when you recognize a very important truth: you need them more than they need you.

So – think about what you can do to make *them* successful – not the other way around. To paraphrase John F. Kennedy, "Ask not what they can do for you. Ask what you can do for your team!"

MISTAKE #2: THROWING YOUR WEIGHT AROUND BEFORE THROWING YOUR "WAIT" AROUND

New leaders are often so enthusiastic about their new authority that they start barking out marching orders – "Do this! Do that!" because, well, they can. They have what's known as "positional power." People will do almost anything they tell them to do, because people can be motivated by fear. Just not for long.

My suggestion? *Slow down to go fast.* Take time to get to know your staff, their strengths and weaknesses, and the issues. Spend more time listening than talking. Earn their trust before you begin to make sweeping changes.

MISTAKE #3: PAYING ATTENTION TO THE BIG PICTURE AND IGNORING THE SMALL STUFF

As you take charge, it's natural to sharpen your focus on the big picture – your vision, where you want to take the team, your goals and objectives. It's important work and cannot be overlooked. But just as important to your team is what most people call the "small stuff."

- They want to know how you like to operate day by day
- How do you feel about being called after hours?
- What should someone do if they strongly disagree with a pending decision you've made, or if they feel you are about to make a mistake?
- How do you like to get information – in person, on the phone, or by email?
- Is your door always open, or do you prefer people set up appointments to talk to you?
- Do you have some pet peeves that people should know about?

You get the idea.

Everyone has to learn how to work with you (just as much as you have to learn to work with them). Save them the trial-and-error approach that only reveals your preferences when people guess wrong, and let them know as much of your so-called "small stuff" as quickly as you can.

If you haven't yet read Chapter Two about holding a Transition Meeting, now might be a good time.

MISTAKE #4: IGNORING THE POWER OF SYMBOLISM

When Tom, a new General Manager for a furniture rental company, came on board, he soon learned that people had been complaining for months about the poor conditions in the employee restroom.

Within 24 hours, before he'd met most of the staff, Tom had the restroom cleaned, repaired and freshly painted. At his first all-hands meeting people were already buzzing about the new leader who demonstrated he cared, he would listen, and he would take action.

Don't ignore the power of a symbolic act. Listen, look around, and find the "employee restroom" you can fix immediately.

MISTAKE #5: CONFUSING CHANGE WITH TRANSITION

As William Bridges points out in *Managing Transitions*, there's a huge difference between change and transition. *Change* is external – it happens to you, while transitions are internal – it happens inside you. *Transition* has three phases – letting go, navigating a "neutral zone," and new beginnings.

Change starts at a beginning, and it's often memorialized by a date. When they put you in charge it was probably announced as a change. "Please join me in congratulating (insert your name here) as the new manager of the department, effective (insert your date here.)"

Transition, on the other hand, starts with an ending – a process of letting go of the way things were.

"We're getting a new manager! What does that mean?" (Remember, WIIFM – what's in it for me?)

You may have become the new manager on October 1st. But in reality, you really become the new manager once people have shifted from letting go of your predecessor, with all of his or her strengths and liabilities, and worked their way through the ambiguity, anxiety, and confusion of the neutral zone, until at last they emerge into a place of accepting you as the new boss. That can take weeks or even months – especially if this internal process is ignored.

There's no way to circumvent the fact that people have to let go of something before they can embrace what's new. If you ignore the dynamics of transition, you will push people's resistance underground. That's why people spend time at the proverbial water cooler discussing all the changes in the organization.

Even if your arrival is the most exciting event imaginable, pay conscious attention to how people are managing their transition – not just what they're saying about the change. Help them let go of the past by:

- Understanding who is giving up what
- Finding ways to honor the past with a ritual or ceremony to mark the endings
- Getting the team to think of ways to bring the best of the past into the future
- Remembering that change and transition often mean more work for a while as you and the team take measure of one another

- Creating an environment where people are safe to express their concerns, fears, misgivings, hopes and aspirations

- Communicating often about what is changing, and what isn't

CHAPTER FOUR

Five Management Habits You Don't Want to Develop

A lament that can hit too close to home suggests that "If you're not a part of the solution, you're part of management!"

Ouch.

There are many things that managers do which will inevitably make things worse. Here's my Top Five list of things you'll want to avoid:

1. Triangulating with people on your staff
2. Delivering negative consequences for good performance
3. Delivering positive consequences for poor performance
4. Procrastinating over performance shortfalls
5. Misusing a rating scale on a performance review

TRIANGULATING WITH STAFF

A problem we all wrestle with is gossip. Malicious gossip can soon poison morale within your team. A common form of gossip occurs when one person has an issue with another person, and talks to a third person about it.

When managers are the "third person," it's called *triangulation*. A staff person comes to you to complain about someone else. You find yourself either eager to help or perhaps just wanting the problem go away, and you begin to engage in the conversation. As it goes back and forth, the two of you are soon triangulating about a third person – who isn't there to present his or her point of view.

It may seem like a harmless conversation, or even like a well-meaning coaching session from the manager, but it's modeling exactly the kind of behavior you don't want in your department.

It's talking behind the third person's back. And if it's okay to do in the manager's office, why wouldn't it be okay for anyone to do it with anyone else?

When this happens to you, nip it in the bud. Instead of continuing the conversation, point out that the two of you are now triangulating, and shift the conversation to help your staff person prepare to take the issue directly to person with whom he or she has the problem.

Do not take sides. If the person with the issue wants help or practice delivering their message to the third person, be a neutral sounding board. Ask questions like:

- What do you want the other person to do?
- Why do you think this person is behaving this way?
- What is stopping you from taking this directly to the other person?
- What outcome would you like after you speak with the other person?

When you find yourself becoming seduced by triangulation, turn it into a coaching opportunity. Make sure the person who's brought the issue to you leaves with the responsibility to take it directly to the third person.

DELIVERING A NEGATIVE CONSEQUENCE FOR DESIRED PERFORMANCE

You might find yourself one day scratching your head and wondering why your team isn't stepping up to the plate to "give 110%." One thing you might want to consider is whether you're inadvertently giving them negative consequences when they perform how you'd like them to perform. Here's how that happens:

- An employee makes a problem-solving suggestion at a brain-storming meeting is immediately tasked with the responsibility to head up a task team to solve the problem, whether or not she has the time to do so.

- An overworked employee who is great at getting things done under pressure is the first one the manager delegates the next unexpected assignment.

- The employee who manages her time well and completes assignments on time is "rewarded" with sarcastic comments about whether she has enough work to do.

Behavior is a function of consequence. We do things (we "behave"), and stuff happens as a result (the "consequences"). Then we modify what we do, based on the consequences we've experienced.

You must be careful that when your employees perform in ways you want them to perform (such as offering ideas at ideas at a brainstorming, working with grace under pressure, or demonstrating good task management skills) not to deliver a negative consequence. Otherwise, over time you will see less of the desired behavior.

DELIVERING A POSITIVE CONSEQUENCE FOR POOR PERFORMANCE

Howard often comes to staff meetings late. Jack rarely turns in production reports on time. Mary has a poor attitude, constantly bad-mouthing her co-workers, gossiping about others, and putting in a minimum effort.

Why? Perhaps in part because their manager is actually *rewarding* their poor performance by giving each of them a positive consequence, probably without even knowing it.

If Howard's boss ignores his tardiness and doesn't address the issue, he actually rewards Howard with more free time to pursue other interests – a positive consequence.

If Jack's boss finds a work-around to overcome the problem of late reports, he relieves him of any deadline tension – a positive consequence.

If Mary's boss is uncomfortable with difficult conversations, he won't confront her about her behavior directly. She gets a positive consequence for poor behavior – the freedom from being held accountable for her performance.

If you must confront poor performance, begin by asking yourself whether you've been contributing to the problem by inadvertently providing a positive consequence for unwanted behavior. Change the consequences, and you will change the behavior.

PROCRASTINATING OVER PERFORMANCE SHORTFALLS

After working with hundreds of managers, I've concluded the most popular strategy to deal with poor performance is procrastination. They put off doing something about it, hoping it will fix itself.

There's actually a good psychological reason many people procrastinate. *Sometimes it works.* Sometimes people do change their ways all on their own and improve their performance.

We are all subject to a fundamental principle of behavior called the law of intermittent reinforcement, which is quite a mouthful. This means that we will engage in a behavior over and over, if we are *occasionally* and *unpredictably* rewarded for that behavior.

For instance, we'll play slot machines, because now and then, in a pattern we can't predict, we'll be a winner. The game would hold no interest if we knew that it paid out every 26th time, for example. It's the unpredictability of the reward that keeps us coming back.

It's the same with procrastination. Every now and then, it pays off. We put off doing a report for a long time, and occasionally the need to do that report changes – it's no longer needed. Thank goodness we procrastinated!

It's understandable that managers put off confronting poor performance because it might get better on its own, but what you must realize is that more often than not, procrastination will only make it worse.

Remember, when you don't confront poor behavior, you're actually supplying a positive consequence for poor performance.

If someone isn't performing to your standards, don't hesitate. Raise the issue. Coach the employee. Hold them accountable. A weed is much easier to pick when it first sprouts than when it gets larger and stronger.

MISUSING A RATING SCALE ON A PERFORMANCE REVIEW

When I first begin working with an organization, I often ask people what's the most important issue that company is currently facing. One that gets raised frequently is "Performance Reviews." Here are some of the problems they identify:

- Not everyone is getting them
- They aren't delivered on time
- The form is terrible
- We're just changing to a new system, and no one understands it
- They are a meaningless process that doesn't add value

But the biggest complaint of all about performance reviews? *My manager games the rating system.*

How is this done?

I remember one manager who told his team, "I never give anyone a 5 (on a 5 point scale) for anything. No one is that good." But how can that be fair, when other managers in the organization use the whole scale?

Other managers have "central tendency." With that same five point scale, they assign a 3 when they can't really decide the appropriate value. They average the number.

Others consistently rate higher than other managers in the organization. Sure, that feels good to their team, but it's still unfair to people in other departments. They may rate high just to avoid having to tell someone he's not cutting it. They have a tendency to be lenient. Whatever their reason, their ratings are not fairly developed.

Still others have the opposite problem: severity. Not just a matter of never using the top of the scale, these managers consistently assign lower ratings (for similar performance outcomes) than do other managers.

Let's face it. Performance evaluation forms are often fraught with problems. Don't let the rating scale be one of yours. Use the whole scale, and evaluate as fairly and accurately as you can.

Part Two: Your New Role

Just what are the expectations of managers in contemporary organizations? What's the "job description" for managers, anyway? Unfortunately, many managers learn how to be managers by absorbing and incorporating the bad habits of their own managers. They emerge as managers with old, ineffective management belief systems.

In the Quick Start chapters ahead, we'll "compare and contrast" management work and leadership, explore why the best managers take 100% accountability for the work of their team (while giving away most of the credit), present some ideas about honor, humility and humor, and show you how to develop your own powerful "elevator speech" which can guide you - and your staff - through difficult times.

CHAPTER FIVE

Can You Do Things Right
While You're Doing The Right Things?

I magine the following classified ad:

Wanted: Someone with good technical skills, savvy organizational skills, and great people skills. Successful candidate will be expected to be a role model, a trainer, a facilitator, a hero, a coach, a drill sergeant, a teacher, a cheerleader, and a mentor (although not necessarily in this order). Long hours, frequent headaches, and very little glory. If you enjoy meeting a challenge, call 1-800-MANAGER to arrange for an interview.

Would you apply?

THE TRADITIONAL VIEW OF MANAGEMENT

What is your understanding of the role of a manager? Traditionally, the manager was said to have four critical responsibilities: planning, organizing, directing, and controlling a work unit. This model led to the understanding that managers were supposed to:

- Get results through *compliance*
- Create strong *followers* who had a healthy respect for authority
- Ensure that employees followed *policy* and *procedure*

- Implement *orders from those above* them in the organization
- Be *responsible* for the actions of the team or department
- Be excellent at the *technical work* performed by the unit
- *Control* people in order to produce the highest possible output

THE CONTEMPORARY VIEW OF MANAGEMENT

Today, there's a more robust understanding of the role of the manager, which encompasses leadership skills as well. In your new position, you will be expected to:

- Get results by gaining the team's *commitment*
- Develop future *leaders*, not just followers
- Manage by *values*, not simply policies and procedures
- Accept and *embrace your leadership*, rather than passing the buck to those above you in the organization
- Have excellent "*people*" skills to complement your technical skills
- *Empower* people to produce the highest possible output

MANAGER OR LEADER?

There's a lot being written in recent years comparing and contrasting managers and leaders as though one has to choose between being one or the other. Warren Bennis, who's perhaps the most prolific writer on this subject, led the charge when he wrote, "Most organizations are over-managed and under-led."

Here are the differences he sees between the two:

1. Leaders focus on *people*; managers focus on *systems*

2. Leaders inspire *trust*; managers rely on *control*

3. Leaders *challenge* the status quo, managers *accept* the status quo

4. The leader is his *own person*; the manager is a classic *good soldier*

5. Leaders do the *right things*; managers do *things right*

I have enormous respect for Bennis, but I believe the distinction he makes between leaders and managers is no longer such a sharp divide. In your new role, you have to do both. You must learn to manage, and you must never forget you're a leader as well – not just a good soldier who does the right things.

Peter Block, in his book *The Empowered Manager*, nailed it when he described three choices he believes every manager faces when confronting critical issues.

1. You must choose between maintenance and greatness.

2. You must choose between caution and courage.

3. You must choose between dependency and autonomy.

You can work hard to keep everything "running smoothly," or you can become a monomaniac on a mission and lead your team to heights they've barely imagined.

You can be careful and prudent, with a well-thumbed policy and procedure manual always at your side, or you can choose to do "the right thing" when the issue demands a solution that can't be boxed in by past practices in the organization.

You can hide behind "upper management" and advocate that their decisions are always right, or you can use your own best judgment and take some risks.

Block is hardly suggesting that managers become mavericks who ignore policy, disregard directives from above, or sabotage the on-going mission of the organization.

He's pointing out that as a manager there will be times when you are called on to truly *lead*. In those moments, when you're faced with something that puts you and your team on the spot – you can choose to lie low, err on the side of caution, and follow orders (knowing you're letting an opportunity slip through your fingers that could change everything) or you can take the leap into the unknown, lead your team into uncharted territory and make a difference.

Nordstrom's, a department store with billions of dollars in annual sales, attributes much of its success because one fundamental employee policy: *always use your own best judgment.*

Then there's the "job description" of a manager at Nordstrom's. It's just two words: *teach judgment.*

That might be the best mental model of what a manager/leader is today.

Welcome to your new assignment.

CHAPTER SIX

What Part of *2 + 2 = 4* Belongs to You?

Here's one of the most important fundamental organizational principles you need to know:

"What" flows down, and "How" flows up.

What needs to happen is primarily a leadership responsibility, and how to make it happen is primarily the responsibility of individual contributors.

Here are some "what" examples:

- We need a new strategy to increase sales by 10%
- The system we use to capture citizen complaints is not working - let's fix it
- We need to get buy-in from three other departments to make this work

The leader's primary job is to determine the goal or direction and define it clearly to everyone on the team. Furthermore, the boss sets the parameters. "We need to figure out how to land that new client – and we must find a creative solution within our budget."

Delivering these "what" messages sends information down.

Let's pretend you're the new boss of the metaphorical Math Department. After giving it careful thought, you've decided today's "goal" for your team is 4. Four what? Four anything. You want the team to "achieve" 4.

As far back as you can remember, when you aimed for 4, you did it this way:

$$2 + 2 = 4$$

Simple. To be clear, 4 is the "what," and 2 + 2 is the "how."

Now you're the boss, and you want 4. You call everyone together, and let them know. "Folks, today we need to achieve 4." You're confident – you've got a talented group.

Off scurries your team, eager to take on the challenge and make their boss happy. Later that day, each comes to you to give you a status update.

Jim says, "I added 2 plus 2 and got 4." You beam.

Cindy says, "I added 1 plus 3 and got 4." You grimace slightly, but no matter. She got 4.

Ted says, "I took 7, subtracted 3, and got 4." *Uh oh.* Ted's wasting resources.

And Suzanne says, "I began with 1.5 and added 3.5. I'm stuck at 5." Now this is a problem – she's using *fractions* and not even getting to 4!

Many a manager would put on their *Serious Face*, grabbed a marker, and direct everyone's attention to the white board.

"Look, people, the goal is 4. FOUR! Only three of you got there, and only one used the standard formula we've used for years. One of you freelanced just a bit but was lucky to get there, one used way too many resources to get there, and one of you got too creative – and didn't even get to the goal. This is unacceptable!"

At that point, many a manager would become Micromanager – able to stomp out creativity, ownership, and commitment with a single command. Don't make that mistake.

Consider this:

> *The ideal manager is*
> *hands-off whenever possible, and*
> *hands-on whenever needed.*

Too hands-off, and you'll be seen as aloof, uncaring, and disinterested. Too hands-on, and you'll start to micromanage. That's where too many managers drift. They become Micromanagers.

Recall the opening principle: "what" should flow down, and "how" should flow up. Let them know the goal, clarify any parameters (use whole numbers, for example) and let them figure out how. That's their job. Let them do it.

You may even learn, as the Math Manager, 2 + 2 is an out-of-date method. Your competitors have found that 1 + 3 is more effective. Some are even exploring

3 + 1, or even – perish the thought, 4 – 0 or 4 + 0. And one is experimenting with a completely new method which uses fractions.

If you let your people determine the "how," you'll increase energy, produce fresh thinking, and commitment to achieving the goal.

Having stretched this metaphor well beyond what is prudent, let me close with this thought. When you adhere to the principle of "what" flows down, and "how" flows up, you will discover opportunities to coach your team to determine the way forward, the "how," without telling them how to do it.

Good coaching isn't about *telling* someone exactly what they should do, but rather is a *process* of helping people discover it for themselves. That's how you create stronger employees. Here are some questions you can use as the centerpiece of a good coaching conversation:

1. To achieve this goal, what do you think we should do?

2. What do you think would happen if we did it that way?

3. What could go wrong, and how could we deal with that?

CHAPTER SEVEN

Take the Blame and Give Away the Credit

When I was a young salesperson moving through a management training program, I came to believe I was really hot stuff. I was told how well I was doing many times; I consistently produced some great numbers, and I heard hints that I was at the top of the list of candidates to open a new facility in a new city – a plum assignment.

With two weeks to go until my training would be complete, I was sent to Denver to work with Pam, perhaps the best Sales Manager in the company. I was there to learn whatever I could from her before getting my first management assignment.

I arrived and was instantly inspired. I watched intently as Pam handled a personnel crisis that had erupted while she drove to the airport to pick me up. Her "grace under pressure" was incredible.

The next day, Pam asked me to accompany an outside sales rep for the day. As Tim and I made his sales calls, it became apparent to me that there were several things Tim was doing wrong that I could fix. (I wasn't "hot stuff" for nothing, after all!) I spent the day "coaching" Tim and arrived back at the office feeling spent but basking in the glow of having helped someone.

How wrong I was!

I walked into Pam's office and was told that I had a phone call from Art, the National Sales Manager. Certain he'd called to congratulate me (once again) for a job well done, I was stunned when he opened the conversation with this: "Gary, what were you thinking? What gives you the right, let alone the authority, to usurp Pam's leadership and try to 'manage' her employee?

"You've got 48 hours to make it right. If you can't do that, you're certainly NOT going to open the new facility, and you may not even graduate from the Manager-In-Training Program."

Whoa! Talk about being red faced!

I hung up, sat with myself for a few minutes, and then went to see Pam. I explained as best I could why I had done what I had done, and I apologized. I was sheepish, embarrassed, and repentant.

What Pam did next has stayed with me for the rest of my career. She told me she understood my account, she accepted my apology, and then she added one more thing.

She told me she'd called Art, and taken full responsibility for what had happened. She took the blame.

She took the blame.

She taught me about a concept she called "100% responsibility." She said that she takes full responsibility for everything that happens on her watch. Even when a dispassionate, objective bystander would say it wasn't her fault, or when she clearly had no control over something that happened.

Why?

Because, she explained, if she believes she is 100% responsible, she acts differently than when she mentally divides the responsibility into parts (hers and mine, for example). She clarified that most people look at relationships as shared responsibilities – such as marriage, often considered a 50/50 deal.

The problem with dividing the responsibility among the stakeholders (the spouses, the team members, etc.) is that when something goes wrong, it is human nature to decide that you did your part (50%?) but the other person didn't do theirs.

And that leads to finger pointing, blame, and covering your butt. Which is not what good leaders do. It's the opposite.

"But how, I asked, are you responsible for what I did today?" I asked.

She told me there could be several things she could have done differently to get a different outcome.

"I could have made my expectations more clear, for instance," she said.

"Or I could have asked you to tell me what lesson you thought you were being given by accompanying my best sales person in the field.

"I could have challenged my own assumptions about you as a trainee, for that matter. After all, I don't really know you all that well."

There were probably a dozen things she could have done differently, she said. Any one of them might have changed the outcome. So, because she hadn't done them, she was 100% responsible for my screw up.

I chewed on that for a long, long time. I came to realize that her taking responsibility for a poor outcome didn't relieve me of my own responsibility, but it did make me want to follow her anywhere. As the saying goes, I was ready to walk off a bridge had she asked.

GIVE AWAY THE CREDIT

Let's talk about giving away the credit. Bear Bryant, the longtime coach of the Alabama Crimson Tide who retired with more wins than any other coach before him put it best: "There's just three things I'd ever say (about being in charge): If anything goes bad, I did it. If anything goes semi-good, then we did it. If anything goes real good, then you did it. That's all it takes to get people to win football games for you."

> *"If anything goes bad, I did it.*
> *If anything goes semi-good, we did it.*
> *If anything goes real good, then they did it."*

That's taking the blame and giving away the credit. It seemed to work for Bear Brant. In his 38 seasons he had 37 winning seasons and participated in a total of 31 post–season bowl games, including 24 consecutively at Alabama. Bryant won 15 bowl games, including eight Sugar Bowls. Over his career, with four universities, he compiled a record of 323 wins, 85 losses, and 17 ties.

That's someone who deserves a lot of credit.

CHAPTER EIGHT

The "H" in Leadership

G reat leaders are often described as visionaries who can see and articulate a compelling future for the rest of us. Great stuff, that. But there's more to the story of what makes a "great" leader.

Without exception, all of the great leaders I've had the privilege to work with brought three qualities to the table which start with the same letter: honor, humility, and humor. They acted with honor, they were humble, and they remembered to poke fun at themselves, especially in difficult times.

HONOR

Only a sociopath truly misunderstands honor. Everyone else gets it – but some choose to abandon it. "He has honor if he holds himself to an ideal of conduct though it is inconvenient, unprofitable, or dangerous to do so," said Walter Lippmann.

Acting with honor is taking the high road. It's "doing right when no one else is looking," as Henry Ford put it. William Safire added, "The right to do something does not mean that doing it is right."

If you need someone to remind you not to cheat on your expense reports, or fudge your activity reports, or misrepresent your team's status updates, these few paragraphs about honor aren't going to matter.

As Zig Ziglar noted, "When a company or an individual compromises one time, whether it's on price or principle, the next compromise is right around the corner."

If you don't live to a high moral standard, you don't belong in a leadership position. It's that simple.

HUMILITY

What fascinates me about humility is that it's about having a disposition to be thinking of others – not yourself. Leaders cannot be humble by trying to be humble – they are seen as having humility when they seek not just to lead but (mostly) to serve.

I find that many people regard being humble as a demonstration of weakness when in fact it is the opposite. The truly humble leader, who gives away the credit when things go well, but owns the accountability when they don't, is the one who demonstrates strength.

David Packard, the co-founder of Hewlett-Packard, has said, "You shouldn't gloat about anything you've done; you ought to keep going and find something better to do."

Bruna Martinuzzi, author of *The Leader as a Mensch: Becoming the Kind of Leader People Want To Follow* writes, "An interesting dichotomy is that, often, the higher people rise, the more they have accomplished, the higher the humility index. Those who achieve the most brag the least, and the more secure they are in themselves, the more humble they are."

HUMOR

Effective leaders also have the ability (and the willingness) to laugh at themselves. They take their work seriously, but themselves lightly. They can break the tension in the room with a remark that points out the irony, or even the insanity, of what's going on.

I was facilitating a large conference for a company which was in the midst of some very serious challenges from competitors. Because was a feeling of "doom and gloom" throughout the organization, a conference had been called to get everyone in the same room and give them the latest information. The grim truth: if they didn't turn things quickly, there would soon be no company to turn around.

It was serious stuff.

The conference was set to open. We were in a huge ballroom with several hundred employees gathered. The buzz wasn't exactly empowering. Far from it. The first two speakers gave some heavy PowerPoint presentations, sucking most of oxygen out of the room. Everyone looked like someone had just died.

It was time for Jim, the CEO, to come to the front of the room and address the crowd. But where was he? As the facilitator, I was getting nervous. He hadn't arrived before the conference, he hadn't mingled with the group, and (most important to me, at least) he hadn't even met with me that morning to go over the final agenda for the event. And now he wasn't even there!

As the last of the first three speakers (all senior executives) began to wind down, my heart rate began to speed up. *Where was Jim?*

As the third speaker concluded his remarks, the room grew silent. I didn't know what to do. Jim was supposed to simply be standing on the sidelines waiting his turn to speak. But there was no Jim. And no way for me to gracefully leave the stage and go look for him.

The silence continued. It seemed like several minutes, but it was probably only one or two. Suddenly a door to the ballroom flung open, and in bounded someone wearing a Mickey Mouse costume.

What on earth? I wondered.

"Mickey" wove through the crowd and made his way to the stage. Everyone was taken aback. What was going on?

He found his way to the lectern, and gazed out over the audience. Taking the microphone, he said, "For those of you who don't know me, I'm Jim, and I'm the CEO of this Mickey Mouse outfit!" Only then did he remove his headpiece.

Laughter rolled over the crowd. They were stunned, surprised and delighted. The mood shifted immediately as Jim began to speak. I watched in amazement as he delivered a very sober, compelling presentation, without notes, and without any slides or other visual aids, about what was going on in the company. And he did it wearing his Mickey Mouse costume throughout. He set the expectations for the conference. (Actually, it would be more accurate to say he "re-set" the expectations for the conference.)

He concluded by reminding everyone of this compelling notion: "Our mission is important. Let's take it seriously. But ourselves? Let's take ourselves lightly. Life's too short."

Long story short: participants were jazzed, the conference was an enormous success; the company revised it's strategy, and the rest is history.

Humor can inspire, relieve tension, and motivate others. It recognizes that we're all in this together, and if we can pause now and then to lighten up, we'll enjoy our experience all the more.

CHAPTER NINE

The Manager of Joy

Imagine you're sitting in the middle row on an airplane, preparing for a flight from Austin to Denver. You settle in and glance at the passenger on your left, thinking a good conversation would help pass the time. You say to him, "Hi, I'm Bill. What do you do?"

He says, "I'm Mark. I'm an accountant." Ah, fascinating, you think. Your stereotype of "bean counters" kicks in and alarm bells start ringing in your head. Maybe you'll pass. Wisely, you keep this sarcasm to yourself.

So you turn to the woman on your right, asking, "Hi, I'm Bill, what do you do?"

She says, "Hi, I'm Judy. I show people how, using three simple steps, they can retire in less than ten years, starting wherever they're at, and then live anywhere they want in the world."

Say what?

Who are you going to talk to the rest of the flight?

Yep – you're going to talk to Judy. In fact, your next question is likely to be, "How do you do that?" Oh, by the way, Judy's also an accountant.

This is about elevator speeches – what they are, why you need them, and how to create them. Takes a bit of work but it's well worth the effort. And now, as a new manager, you have the perfect opportunity to craft your own.

An elevator speech is a short description of who you are and what you do which could be delivered in the time it takes to ride an elevator several floors – perhaps 30 seconds. In fact, it's sometimes called the 30-second speech. It contains several key elements.

- It identifies *who you are*
- It describes *what you do*
- It identifies who benefits from what you do – your unique *"value proposition"*

It does all of this in a way that makes it nearly impossible for the listener not to say, "Oh? How do you do that?" or "Oh? Tell me more!"

The obvious uses for an elevator speech are at conferences, conventions, professional meetings or introductions to potential clients or customers. When someone approaches Bill and says, "What do you do?" he can respond with his elevator speech, rather than trotting out the far more typical (and forgettable) response that usually goes like this: "I'm Bill, and I'm the manager of Parks and Recreation for a mid-sized city." Yawn.

All Bill has done is give the other person a name they will soon forget, and a job title that carries with it tired stereotypes I'm sure he'd rather avoid.

But there's an even more important reason to develop your own elevator speech. It reminds you of who you really are – what makes you unique and why you do the things you do.

Let's go back to Judy and hear the rest of her elevator speech. Remember how it begins?

"Hi, I'm Judy. I show people how, using three simple steps, they can retire in less than ten years, starting wherever they're at, and then live anywhere
they want in the world."

That's called the hook.

It has but one purpose – to capture your interest – to get you to "bite." When it works, you'll say "Tell me more!" When it doesn't, you'll say "Gee, that's interesting." And then you'll crack the book you brought along on the plane and start reading.

Once Judy gets her listener to ask for more, she can finish her elevator speech. Listen to what she says:

"I work with professionals who may not be financially savvy or lack the time or interest to design a nearly fail-safe retirement plan.

"Often, this begins with a two hour meeting during which we determine where they are right now, where they'd like to be when they retire, and what they're doing to make that happen.

"Next, I teach them three simple tools which will get their finances in order and help them make some adjustments in their savings, spending and investment habits.

"Afterwards, we meet for an hour or so every six months to keep on track.

"My specialty is working with professionals who are deeply in debt and worried they may never be able to retire comfortably."

Wow. When can I make an appointment?

Judy's elevator speech is compelling because while it might seem to be about her, it's really about her listener. She's responding with what we all want to know: what's in it for me?

Having heard Judy's speech, Bill wants one of his own. How does he develop it?

1. First, Bill should write down the services he (and his department) provide.

2. Next, he should translate those services into benefits his clients or customers enjoy.

3. After that, he should work on his hook – what will get someone to say "tell me more!"?

After a bit of word-smithing and some false starts, he might come up with a hook that sounds like this:

"Hi, my name is Bill.
I'm the Manager of Joy for a mid-sized city."

Say what? The manager of joy? What's that? Tell me more!

Bill can then go on to say:

"I'm in charge of the Parks and Recreation Department for (Bill's city). My team of outstanding park and recreation specialists create joyful community experiences for people throughout our city who enjoy our parks and the programs we offer.

"We know we create joy because people tell us that all the time – from parents of pre-schoolers to senior citizens. In fact, we've just been awarded a national 'Playful City' award.

"We're always looking for ways to create more joy, so if you have any ideas, I'd love to hear them."

Wouldn't you want to spend some time with Bill?

THE BEST REASON FOR AN ELEVATOR SPEECH

Earlier I said that elevator speeches are useful at conferences, conventions, professional meetings or introductions to potential clients or customers. But there's an even more important reason to develop your own elevator speech. *It reminds you of who you really are – what makes you unique and why you do what you do.*

Once Bill has committed his elevator speech to memory, and has used it so often it's become a natural response, it becomes a compass for him throughout his busy days. When he's buried in a report he's writing and feeling weary, when he's headed for another meeting he wishes he could avoid, when he comes home tired and worn out and wondering why he does what he does, he will recall the hook in his elevator speech: *"I'm the manager of joy."*

That's why he does what he does, and why it's so important. People are counting on him – from his staff to the public. Everyone wants more joy.

It becomes a mantra that he uses to manage his staff. He can use it's central premise – bringing joy to people – to inspire his staff. He can use it to make decisions – which choice will bring the most joy to our customers? He can use it to modify systems and adjust procedures.

Spend the time to develop an elevator speech. When you or your staff begins to lose sight of the forest as you stare at the tree in front of you, it can shift your focus. You can approach that next boring meeting with renewed energy, as Bill does – after all, he's the Manager of Joy.

Part Three: Your New Team

As you will soon see, becoming a manager isn't all about you, except perhaps to you. It's about your team.

We'll begin with some Quick Start chapters on how to think about the people you're about to manage. I'll compare managing people with operating a floor sander - there are real parallels between the two! Next, you'll get two different (but complimentary) ways to think about the kinds of people who might be on your team, and how to manage each type.

You'll learn what your team wants from you more than anything else, and a fantastic technique to get folks to meet your performance expectations without falling back on reviews or disciplinary action.

CHAPTER TEN

Managing People Is Like Operating a Floor Sander

Years ago, I worked for a summer in the maintenance department of my high school. One day my supervisor asked me if I'd ever operated a floor sanding machine, which looks like a giant vacuum cleaner. I'd never seen one, but with the hubris of youth, I said, "Sure!"

"Good," he said. "Every two years we have to strip the gymnasium floor and refinish it. This is the year, today's the day, and now you're the guy who's gonna strip it."

I was dispatched to the gym where I found the machine already in place. How hard could this be? I asked myself. I plugged it in and turned it on.

Instantly the sander began revolving at high speed, and the machine gyrated about the floor as though it had an evil plan. Instinctively I grabbed the handles harder and began pushing down to control the machine. BIG mistake.

The harder I tried to control the machine, the more it dragged me around the floor and gouged the hardwood. Panicking, I lost sight of the on/off switch. It wasn't until the machine (on it's own – I swear!) moved near an electrical outlet that I managed to yank the plug from the outlet and stop the monster. With dismay I realized that several square feet of the floor were close to ruin.

After sheepishly bringing my boss to the gym, I was given a lesson in floor sanding. Turns out a very light touch – an almost Zen-like mental state makes operating the machine easy. It rebels when you try to "control" it by bearing down on it, and it shines when you allow it to do its job.

Many years later I realized I'd been given a good metaphor for managing people. Turns out, even though they are (obviously) not machines, they respond about the same way to their "operator" – their boss. Push down hard, and try to control everything, and they'll take you all over the floor.

"Leadership," said Dwight Eisenhower, "is the art of getting someone else to do something you want done because he wants to do it." He's right.

WE DO WHAT WE DO FOR ONE OF TWO REASONS:

1. We think we *have to*.

2. We know we *want to*.

As the boss, you're going to be making plans, setting priorities, making decisions, and assigning projects to your staff. You can instill fear or foster desire. It's really that simple. You can go for *compliance*, or you can go for *commitment*.

Unlike a floor sander, people will do things they think they have to do – but only to a point. We've all worked for a boss who said things like:

"It's my way or the highway."
"We don't pay you to think. We pay you to perform."
"When I want your opinion, I'll give it to you."

I'd like to say these days are long over, but sadly, they're not. There are plenty of bosses who "rule by fear." Their power comes from their position, not their vision or passion. They'll get superficial results – but eventually, their "gym floor" will be gouged, nicked, and scarred.

Managers who create environments of support, commitment, a sense of ownership, recognition, and a strong belief in the incredible potential of their people will prevail in the long run.

The lesson is simple: if you push too hard to control your people, they will never achieve much. If you guide them, coach them, support them, and believe in them, they'll take you – and your organization – to places you can hardly imagine.

CHAPTER ELEVEN

The Good, the Bad, and the Ugly

If you manage long enough, you'll encounter three kinds of people: those who *support* you, those who *sabotage* you, and those who *split* (but never really leave). Much of this has to do with how you manage them.

SUPPORTERS

Most people, day in and day out, support the aims of the organization, the goals of your team, and you. They come to work wanting to do what used to be called an "honest day's work." While they may occasionally be distracted, they believe in the organization, and they set about trying to do their part.

They are not blind followers. They might have disparate viewpoints, different opinions, and disagreements over strategy, policy or assignment. But they are solid contributors, good team players – people you can count on to get the job done.

Supporters do the job asked of them because they want to do so. Treat them well, and they will reward you and your organization with their best effort.

Treat them poorly, consider them simply "human resources," or parts of a machine, and they will lose their confidence in you. Stop treating them with respect, stop listening to them and asking for their help, and they will not remain supporters very long.

SABOTEURS

Then there are those who sabotage the organization, their team, and you. Rather than working for the organization, they work against it.

Sabotage has two meanings: deliberate destruction, and taking action to hinder. You've seen examples of the first type on the news – workplace violence and vandalism. What's more subtle – and more common – is the second type. There are countless ways to take action to hinder: give less than 100% effort, take frequent absences, miss assignments or meetings (or forget them), or bad-mouth people and/or decisions, just to name a few.

Another form of sabotage that's much harder to recognize and eradicate is called *malicious compliance*, which shows up when employees do exactly what they've been told to do – nothing more, and nothing less. This allows them to protect themselves (better known as CYA) by being able to say, "What's the problem? I did exactly what you told me to do!"

An example: employees who have time cards know there's usually a few minutes grace period for each end of the shift that allow them to get credit for a full eight hours. Saboteurs are those who habitually clock in a few minutes late, and clock out a few minutes early – just within the policy parameters.

What causes people to become saboteurs? Some of the more common reasons:

- They've become disillusioned with the organization because they don't like what's happening – layoffs, restructuring, changing priorities, budget cuts, etc.

- They've become disenfranchised and disgusted with leadership. Perhaps they've been asked to cut corners, or put into ethical dilemmas, or become the subject of gossip.

- They might simply be overworked, and tired of hearing the old adage, "let's do more with less."

The biggest reason people change from supporters to saboteurs, in my opinion, is bad management. Playing favorites, delivering unfair performance evaluations, not listening, taking people for granted, keeping them in the dark – the list goes on.

SPLIT

The third kind of employee you might encounter has chosen to split – but not to leave. They "retire" on the job. These are the people that don't even have the energy to actively sabotage – they've just given up. We often call them "dead wood."

They manage to stay with the organization, sometimes for years, but they don't really care about the mission, their team, or their boss. They just take up space. How does this happen?

Once again, it's bad management. In this case, it's often the result of not being held accountable for their performance. Often they haven't had an honest performance appraisal in years. There's been no straight talk – no performance improvement plan – no negative consequences for performing poorly. Does this mean they share no responsibility for becoming dead wood? Of course not. They are 100% accountable for their performance – but it couldn't have happened, in my view, had they been properly managed.

What this means to you

When you realize you have saboteurs on your staff – or, heaven forbid, someone who has split without leaving, you must act.

Coach the saboteur, hold him accountable for their behavior, and get him to recommit to the organization.

You must act to remove any dead wood. These folks *can't* be turned around – it's far too late. Begin a termination process. As Andrew Carnegie put it, "There is no use trying to help people who won't help themselves. You cannot push someone up a ladder who is not willing to climb himself."

The good news is that almost everyone is – or wants to be – a supporter. With good coaching, a saboteur can be turned around. Think of your actions as "tough love," and their behavior as a "cry for help."

Great managers rarely have saboteurs, and if they occasionally inherit some dead wood, they take action to remove that person immediately – no matter how difficult.

CHAPTER TWELVE

All Stars and Lost Causes

In the last chapter I grouped employees into three groups – those who support you, those who sabotage you, and those who split. Another model sorts them into *four* categories – the *All Stars*, the *Steady Performers*, the *Marginal Performers*, and the *Lost Causes*. Both constructs are useful. I came by this model many years ago and have been unable to find proper attribution (but if someone can fill me in, I'll be happy to update this chapter in future editions of this book).

Let's take a look at each group:

1. **All Stars** are people who invariably achieve outstanding results well above the standard set for them.

2. **Steady Performers** are people who can be counted on to deliver predictable performance that meets and occasionally exceeds standards.

3. **Marginal Performers** are people who have slipped below standards and are now demonstrating unsatisfactory performance which only occasionally meets standards.

4. **Lost Causes** are people who have given up trying to meet standards, and, by definition, can't be turned around.

ALL STARS

All Stars are rare. I'd guess in most organizations, these are the *crème de la crème*, and comprise perhaps 2-3% of the organization. An All Star is a person who consistently does amazing things that raise the bar beyond what's even thought possible. They are not the "employee of the month." They are the "employee of the year."

All Stars are a unique group of people who, if we're honest about, rarely need much supervision. They combine their talent with passion and set an example that's often astonishing.

Most managers who've had the pleasure and good fortune of having an All Star on their team take very little credit for that person's accomplishments. They realize the achievements were not a result of the manager being a great teacher or mentor, although that may have helped. This level of performance is something that the employee brought to the table on their own and it's a joy to watch and infectious to be around.

If you have an All Star on your team, count your blessings. Odds are you'll need them, and get more from them, than they need you or get from you.

HOW SHOULD YOU MANAGE AN ALL STAR?

Make sure the person really is an All Star. In your honest opinion, are they really part of the top 2-3% of the organization (not just your team)? If they truly are, then thank the universe for giving you the opportunity to have one on your staff.

Manage them with a light hand. If "good managers are hands-on as much as needed, and hands-off as much as possible," err on the side of "hands-off." Give them challenges and direction, yes, but then stand back. You can take it to the bank that they will deliver well above and beyond your expectations – that's the nature of All Stars. And by the way, All Stars like recognition as much as anyone else, but they don't thrive on recognition. They thrive on achievement. They know when they've done the spectacular. Give them recognition when they've earned it, and move on.

Do not succumb to the temptation to raise your standards for everyone else to the level of performance of an All Star. That's unfair, and you're setting up the remainder of your team for failure. Set high, aggressive standards, but do not use the performance of an All Star to determine what you expect from the others. Remember, All Stars are performance freaks!

Prepare yourself for the inevitable: All Stars rarely stand still. They get promoted quickly to bigger challenges, and that may not be within your department or on your team.

Be grateful for any All Stars that come your way, and remember that you may not have them for long.

STEADY PERFORMERS

You want the majority of your team to be Steady Performers, and the odds are they will be. These are the same folks who are Supporters described in Chapter 11, "The Good, The Bad, and The Ugly."

Steady Performers are consistent. They meet performance standards far more often than not. They come to work, day after day, and get the job done.

How should you handle Steady Performers?

Set high, but fair standards. Remember, people will rise or fall to your level of expectation . Expect excellence, and you will get excellence.

As Ken Blanchard put it in his book *The One Minute Manager*, "Catch 'em doing something right." Look for opportunities to recognize and reward good performance. Whether that's a round of applause at a staff meeting, a positive Post-It note attached to a draft of a report they've written and you've reviewed, a simple "thank you!" delivered when it's least expected, make sure you're recognizing their achievements frequently.

If you can, vary their assignments and keep stretching them. Employees thrive when they can engage in work that has meaning, is perceived to make a difference, and facilitates their professional growth. Just because someone is a Steady Performer doesn't mean they want to do the same thing, over and over.

Don't procrastinate when something seems amiss – when they're not their "usual self." Steady Performers do have times when they slip below the performance expectation line you've drawn – we all do. The time for performance coaching (or personal counseling) is when things first start to slip – not later.

Also, don't fall into the habit of making one or two of your Steady Performers your "go to" people every time a crisis hits. Spread the wealth. Develop a whole team of "go to" people. While it can be rewarding to be the "go to" guy, when it's overdone, it reaches a point of diminishing returns. Always turning to the same Steady Performer when you need something done right away or when you need someone to stay late can begin to turn a Steady Performer into a Marginal Performer.

MARGINAL PERFORMERS

The critical thing to remember about Marginal Performers is that *each one was once a Steady Performer*. People do not choose to consistently deliver subpar performance, (except for Lost Causes).

There are two primary reasons people become Marginal Performers:

1. **Something is going on outside of work that has them distracted, worried, or even depressed.** Maybe it's a health issue, or a marital issue. Maybe they've been trying to sell their house without success. Maybe their children are leaving the nest. Perhaps they have parents who need elder care. It can be almost anything, but it's overwhelming them and making it difficult to perform at work. These folks need counseling, and it's your responsibility to see that whatever resources you can make available to them are offered.

2. **Marginal Performers can be created by poor managers.** It begins when a manager chooses to overlook the red flags and warning signs that

occur when a Steady Performer starts to slide. Remember, behavior follows the path of least resistance. If an employee's performance begins to slip beneath the standard you've set, you must do something about it. If you choose to look the other way, or hope that things will correct themselves, or simply procrastinate, you will be telegraphing to this former Steady Performer that it's okay to be consistently under the line.

How should you handle Marginal Performers?

You must have a performance management conversation with them – the sooner the better. You must make them aware that their performance is subpar and needs to be corrected.

Afterwards, look for any and every opportunity to catch 'em doing something right and recognize that effort. Don't wait for everything to be at or above standard. As their performance begins to approach what you expect of them, let them know you've seen the progress and are pleased with it.

Two rules of thumb regarding performance coaching:

1. As a manager, you're going to be involved in formal and informal performance coaching many times. That's a big part of your job. So…

2. Spend at least 80% of your coaching time with Marginal Performers, another 15% of your coaching time with Steady Performers who have temporarily slipped. Do not make the mistake of spending too much of your coaching time on Lost Causes. Don't put it off!

Lost Causes

Just as All Stars comprise 2-3% of an organization, so do Lost Causes. A big mistake many managers make is presuming a Marginal Performer is a Lost Cause. Most aren't – but they can become one, if they are not coached.

So who's a Lost Cause? These are employees who:

- Would have been seen as a Marginal Performer a while back. Unfortunately, management dropped the ball, didn't hold them accountable, and they slipped further and further below standard.
- Have given up, but haven't quit.
- Turn in substandard performance routinely.
- Don't care anymore.
- Have an obviously negative attitude.
- Most important, Lost Causes really don't want to be turned around.

The problem with Lost Causes is not just that their performance is so poor, or even that their negative attitude is distracting if not contagious. It's that they can consume lots of your time!

Lost Causes create four issues for their managers

1. They can seduce well-meaning managers into a long back-and-forth battle to win them over and bring them back into the fold.

2. They consume far more than their share of valuable management time fixing the problems caused by their poor performance.

3. They drag others down. Steady Performers start to wonder why they (the Steady Performers) should continue to give 100% effort. Marginal Performers even more so.

4. Whatever efforts are being made by the manager to address the Lost Cause must be kept confidential, so other team members, in the absence of accurate information, often assume that nothing's being done.

How should you handle Lost Causes?

First, be certain they are truly lost. If there's a track record of performance review, performance plans, and performance management that has failed to result in improved performance, they are a Lost Cause.

If they are lost, they must be terminated. Fired. Let go. There's nothing else to do. Lost Causes cannot be rehabilitated, they cannot be motivated, and they cannot be saved. Termination is often a drawn-out affair, which can be agonizing, but you have no other choice. If you have a Lost Cause, or you've inherited one, you must get them out of the organization.

(Notice I said "organization," not "team." I've yet to see the Lost Cause who can turn things around somewhere else in the organization. Marginal Performers can – and sometimes this is exactly what they need – a fresh start somewhere else in the organization).

Do the right thing, for your team, your organization, and yourself. Work with Human Resources, and start the process to terminate any Lost Causes you have. The alternative is too costly.

Your goal, as manager, is to build a team lucky enough to have the occasional All Star, well populated with Steady Performers, with perhaps the occasional a Marginal Performer who is taking steps to return to steady, dependable performance. And no Lost Causes!

While employees are, in the final analysis, responsible for their own performance and behavior, as manager you have a responsibility to set high standards, reward and recognize those who achieve them, coach those who are falling short, and remove those who are failing and can't be saved.

CHAPTER THIRTEEN

What Does Your Team Want Most?

L et's face it. Being a manager is tough work, but somebody has to do it. And now, that's you.

Maybe you've given some thought to what you want to bring to your new position – the direction you will take the team, the changes you plan to make, the productivity improvements, the cost-savings, and so on. You might have already set some goals.

But have you taken some time to think about what kind of boss you're going to be? Ever wonder what people think are the characteristics of the ideal boss?

The researchers have. They've learned that if you give enough people a piece of paper and ask them to make a list of the qualities they'd like in their manager, you'll get an aggregate list that looks something like this (shown in alphabetical order):

· Career advice

· Consistency

· Fairness

· Knowledge of the field

· Integrity

· Reliability

· Respect

- Support through coaching and feedback
- Teaching and mentoring

WHAT'S THE MOST IMPORTANT THING?

I've left one thing off – and it rises to the top of the collective lists. It's what people value most from their boss.

People want from their boss
the experience – the feeling – of "being heard."

They want to know that when they talk to you, you'll actually listen and "get" their point of view. They don't expect that you'll agree with it all the time; they don't expect to prevail in every dialogue about a decision. But they do want to feel heard.

I find it disappointing that organizations spend millions of dollars every year teaching communication skills to managers and employees alike, and they emphasize:

- How to speak clearly
- Presentation skills
- Writing skills

But they rarely emphasize the most important communication skill of all: listening.

Studies have shown that most folks spend about 9% of their communication time writing, 16% reading, 30% speaking, and 45% listening. Frankly, most of us could benefit from improving our *listening* skills. For those who lead others, it's critical.

MOST PEOPLE HAVE DEVELOPED GOOD "FAKE LISTENING" SKILLS.

Imagine you're at lunch with a group of people and someone is telling a long-winded joke. As your attention fades, you begin thinking about other things. Suddenly, you become aware that everyone is laughing. What do you do?

You laugh, of course! You pretend to have listened the whole time. Nothing wrong with that – it wasn't that important, and you'll probably get away with it – unless the person next to you whispers to you, "I didn't get it. Can you explain the joke?"

Gulp.

But too many managers "fake it" when it really matters. Maybe they have too many things on their mind. Maybe they're up against a deadline. Maybe they think the issue isn't all that important. For whatever reason, they engage in "fake listening" and hope the other person doesn't catch them at it.

But we do. We know. We may not say anything because you're the boss, after all. But we will leave with an unpleasant impression.

CREATING THE EXPERIENCE OF "BEING HEARD"

You need to do three things:

1. *Be fully present.* Make eye contact with the other person. Lean forward. Make good "listening noises" like: "Uh huh." "Go on." "Tell me more."

2. *Paraphrase and summarize* their content. Put what they said into your words.

3. *Reflect back* what you sense they're feeling about the content. You don't have to share that feeling; in fact you may feel quite differently.

The better you are at being present, putting into your own words what you hear them saying, and understanding how they feel about the issue, the more you'll convey the experience of "being heard."

This is authentic listening, or what some call "active listening." It takes more time, and it takes more effort. But it's really pretty simple: you have to actually listen.

If you can do that during those conversations that really matter to the people who work for you, you will be giving them what they want most in a boss – someone who really hears what they're saying. And that will go a long way toward fostering loyalty, honesty, and commitment.

CHAPTER FOURTEEN

The Path of Least Resistance

Have you ever wondered why people keep doing the things they do? Particularly, when they keep doing things you don't want them to do? Simple: they're following the path of least resistance.

I worked with a manager, Carol, who had a problem. Her team was showing up late for staff meetings. At first it wasn't much of an issue, but as time passed, she grew more frustrated. People kept coming late. Carol started doing the following things:

- She delayed starting the meetings until everyone was finally there.

- She made sarcastic comments about punctuality at the beginning of her meetings.

- She occasionally threatened to lock the door of the conference room the next time people were late (but never did).

But the problem just got worse. It reached a point where the Carol herself came late for a meeting, justifying it to the staff by saying, "Well, if you're all going to come late, I might as well do the same."

Ah, sarcasm. Not a compelling leadership tool.

Robert Fritz, in his book *The Path of Least Resistance*, compares the behavior of people to the behavior of rivers.

Rivers always seek the easiest way to get from one point to another – water always flows downhill. People do the same thing. We do what we do because we learn which behaviors produce the least resistance. Put another way, we learn which behaviors lead to the least negative consequences.

Coming late to staff meetings had become a path of least resistance for Carol's staff. The consequences were minor – some sarcasm, an idle threat or two, but nothing ever came of it. To arrive when the meeting was scheduled to start would mean they would have to change their behavior by becoming better time managers and by being more considerate of others. There was almost no reason to do that!

Fritz says that the path of least resistance is determined by an underlying "structure." For the river, this is gravity. For you and me, it's tension. We will look for ways to behave that produce the least amount of tension.

CREATE A NEW PATH WITH A POSTER BOARD, A FELT TIP MARKER, AND SOME SMILEY FACES

The solution for Carol was to change her focus from the undesired behaviors to the underlying structure. She needed to find a way to change that structure and create some tension and make coming to meetings on time the path of least resistance.

How she did that is simply fascinating. Using a simple tool, she was able to get her staff to meetings on time without any official corrective action, employee coaching, written warnings, or any of the usual techniques you're taught in management training. And she did it in less than three weeks.

She used a poster board, a felt tip marker and a stack of sticky "smiley faces."

Carol took the marker to create a simple chart on the poster board. In the first column, she put the names of each of her staff members (including herself). The other columns were headed by the dates of staff meetings. She called the chart Staff Meetings On Time Record. She posted the chart in the conference room where everyone could see it (even other employees, because the conference room was shared with others).

At the next staff meeting, she took note of who had arrived on time. In the cell next to each name, beneath the date of that meeting, she stuck a smiley face for each person who had arrived on time.

That's it. That's all she did.

She did not talk about the chart. She did not tell them she wanted to put a smiley face next to each of their names. Carol did not scold anyone who hadn't earned a smiley face. She simply stuck a smiley in the appropriate cell for each person who was on time.

It was a game changer. After just a couple of meetings, tardy members of the staff began to experience some internal tension – the kind that comes from experiencing a difference between what Fritz calls their "current reality" (a person who's being publicly noticed as tardy and thoughtless) and their "desired reality" (a person who's got a string of happy faces on the chart). No one wanted two or three blank spaces in a row. *By the third week, everyone was on time.*

To get from blank cells to smiley faces meant finding a new path of least resistance, and now, for the first time, it became easier for Carol's staff to come to meetings on time than it was to face the embarrassment of having no smiley face on the chart.

This is crucial: Carol didn't do anything *to her staff* to change their behavior beyond changing their focus on a new "desired reality." She merely changed the path of least resistance. Then human nature took over, and the staff began to modify their behavior almost overnight to meet the new conditions.

BEYOND CHARTS AND SMILEY FACES

I worked for one boss who had a plaque on the wall behind his desk. It said simply, "Results, not excuses." I learned quickly that if I came to Mike with a "reason" my report would have to be late, he didn't say a word. He pointed to his plaque. Being red-faced was not my idea of a path of least resistance. I did whatever it took to get those reports on time.

The story is told that Henry Kissinger hired a bright young intern and assigned him a research project. The intern completed his work and sent it to Kissinger. The next day, there was a note on the report, which had been returned to the intern.

It read, "Is this your best work? H.K."

Mortified, the intern went back to work and redid the project. He turned it in again, and the next day, he got it back – again.

New note: "Is this your BEST work? H.K."

After his third iteration, he gathered his courage and delivered the report personally. Kissinger took it in hand, looked at the intern, and asked, "Is this your best work?"

The intern stood firm. "Yes, sir!" he responded.

"Good," said Kissinger. "*Now I shall read it.*"

The path of least resistance, if you worked for Henry Kissinger, was simple. Always do your best work.

Part Four: Your New Work

Just what does a manager really do?

The following Quick Start chapters explore how and when effective managers involve their team to make better decisions, how to make those tough "it's lonely at the top" decisions, how to help your team reach consensus when you need their full support and commitment, and some great tips on how to conduct staff meetings where actual work gets done.

Meetings that work? What a concept!

CHAPTER FIFTEEN

How to Decide How to Decide

One characteristic all effective managers share is decisiveness. They find the sweet spot between gathering data endlessly and acting rashly. They are neither wishy-washy nor impulsive.

"Be willing to make decisions. That's the most important quality in a good leader," said T. Boone Pickens. "Don't fall victim to what I call the Ready-Aim-Aim-Aim Syndrome. You must be willing to fire."

Being decisive is important, but it is not enough. You must know which decisions should be made by you alone, which should include input from your staff, and which should be delegated to them. A few years ago, my colleague Eric Klein and I published *To Do or Not To Do – How Successful Leaders Make Better Decisions*. This is the Quick Start chapter on better decision-making.

Suppose that you were asked by your boss to make some changes in the budget for your department. This would mean realigning priorities, giving some projects more resources while cutting back on others. All of your staff would be impacted by what you decide the final recommendation would be. How would you choose to reallocate the budget?

Now Hear This!

Knowing that this has the possibility of being an unpopular decision, you might make the decision by yourself without discussing it with your staff. This decision-making style is called *Now Hear This!*

Trial Balloon

You might want to make the decision on your own, but add a "quality control" check *after* you've reached a conclusion, but *before* making it final. You'd gather your staff to discuss the issue, asking them if they could offer any reasons you should modify your recommendations before taking them to the boss. This is a *Trial Balloon* decision.

Buck Stop

You might want to make the decision yourself, but feel that staff input was critical *before* you considered the options. This style is called the *Buck Stop*, named for Harry S Truman's famous expression "the buck stop's here." This is how he came to authorize the use of the atomic bomb against Japan in World War II. He invited a variety of experts – military, political, sociological and others to offer their opinions, and only then made the final decision by himself. Each of these people had the opportunity to influence Truman's choice.

LIFE RAFT

Perhaps you feel that this decision is worth gathering everyone together to seek *consensus* on the best alternatives. While not giving up your accountability for the decision, you would pull the group together and develop a budget recommendation as a team that each member agrees to fully support. We call this style the *Life Raft* because it's a recognition that "we're all in this together." It's the best way to get the team's commitment to the decision by having them shape it and own it.

YOU TELL ME!

A final decision-making alternative is to delegate the issue to the team to resolve, within parameters that you establish. You would call the team together, let them know that the budget must be reworked to create recommendations you can send to your boss, and task them with finding solutions that are within certain parameters.

"We must have an overall reduction of 3%. We can actually increase funding for critical projects, but if we do so, others must be curtailed even further or eliminated. Since you are most familiar with the details on your own projects, work out a plan by Friday describing what our recommendations should be."

This style is known as *You Tell Me!* and is almost a mirror image of *Now Hear This!*

CHOOSING THE MOST APPROPRIATE STYLE

Each of these styles has value, and each is more appropriate for some situations than others. As you broaden your management experience, you'll want to become fluent with all five styles. Too many leaders become comfortable with one or two and never develop their capacity to use the others.

Many a boss barks out too many *Now Hear This!* decisions and struggles with staff support and commitment, while others, in a misguided attempt to be a champion for employee involvement, involve too many people in too many decisions, slowing the team to a crawl.

To add to what Pickens said, the leader who makes too many decisions by himself could be said to have a "Fire! Ready, Aim" mentality. The leader who tries to include everyone too often has a "Ready? Ready? Ready? Aim-Fire" mindset. Neither predisposition is effective.

The trick is finding the balance between deciding on your own, including your team in the process, and delegating decisions to them. *You've got to know how to decide how to decide.*

Eric and I discovered that effective managers were asking themselves three critical questions before consciously choosing whether and how to involve their staff in a given decision:

1. Does this decision call for compliance, or is it a matter that will need their tangible support and commitment?

2. How much time is available to make the decision?

3. How experienced is the team making decisions as a group?

THE FIRST QUESTION:
DO YOU WANT COMPLIANCE OR COMMITMENT?

Now Hear This! and *Trial Balloon* decisions are compliance-centric. That is, they are made with the expectation that the team will implement them because that is the job of the team – to "make it so."

Life Raft and *You Tell Me!* are commitment-centric styles, because as people put their fingerprints on the decision and have the opportunity to shape the final outcome, they are much more likely to be highly supportive. As is often said, they "own the decision."

A *Buck Stop* decision balances compliance and commitment.

THE SECOND QUESTION:
HOW MUCH TIME IS AVAILABLE?

It usually takes a group of people more time to make a decision than one person acting alone. When time is a critical factor, such as during an emergency, managers may need to select from the *Now Hear This!* or *Trial Balloon* end of the continuum. If time is not that pressing a factor, more involvement by the team can be encouraged.

THE THIRD QUESTION:
HOW EXPERIENCED IS THE TEAM?

It's difficult to reach consensus if the team has little experience working together as a team. As a team learns to work together, more decisions can be made by the team.

Successful managers take the third question – team maturity – quite seriously. Knowing that decision quality can rise when there are more people engaged in weighing the options, they see upcoming decisions as opportunities to both *choose a wise course of action* and *develop their team.*

Their confidence in the competence of their team to make decisions as a group will rise as they skillfully facilitate creative dialogue around the conference table.

BE TRANSPARENT

As important as it is to choose the most appropriate style for the decisions you will make, it is equally important to be *transparent* with your staff about that choice.

You've probably been at meetings where the meeting leader framed a discussion about an issue by saying, "We need to get everyone's input on this one. Let's hear your ideas."

People begin offering suggestions, and someone gets busy writing them on the flipchart. Suddenly, it occurs to you – *they already know what they're going to do. This process is a sham!*

It is, so why does it happen? Because unskilled managers want the participants *to feel as though they were involved* – without being authentically involved. They're trying to *fool* their employees into commitment. The truth is that most people would prefer their boss to be honest if the decision is a *Now Hear This!* – even if they would have liked to have given input. Be transparent with your decision-making to let your staff know which style you're applying to a given situation. People do understand that sometimes the boss will make the decision and there is no "vote."

Pretending to include people in the process is a classic mistake that will usually backfire.

IT'S A LEARNING PROCESS

Successful managers weren't born with the knack to use the full spectrum of team-based decision-making styles. They've practiced moving across the continuum until they felt comfortable with every style. As they did so, the quality of their decisions increased as did the confidence of others in their leadership.

Remember, too, this is the Quick Start guide for decision-making. To learn more, get *To Do or Not To Do – How Effective Leaders Make Better Decisions.* I'm told the authors have written a pretty good book.

CHAPTER SIXTEEN

The Four Percent Decision

There will come a time when you have to make a really tough decision, and you must make it alone. It's a classic *Now Hear This!* situation (see Chapter 15). Whatever you choose, some aren't going to like it, some are going to doubt it, and there's a chance that the choice will prove incorrect. You might lose some sleep over it, as you consider – and reconsider – all the options.

Finally, it is time to act. But still you have doubts. What can you do with those nagging doubts?

You can take to heart what Bertrand Russell said, "The whole problem with the world is that fools and fanatics are always so certain of themselves, but wiser people so full of doubts."

You can remember what William Shakespeare wrote: "Modest doubt is the beacon of the wise."

You can follow writer Cynthia Heimel's suggestion: "When in doubt, make a fool of yourself. There is a microscopically thin line between being brilliantly creative and acting like the most gigantic idiot on earth. So what the hell, leap."

But still there's that doubt.

I was told years ago that there is research suggesting that only 4% of our decisions actually make a fundamental difference in the way our lives unfold. I can't swear this is true, and I can't site the research, but my gut tells me that makes sense. In other words, any choice is better than no choice at least 96% of the time.

Perhaps that's why Oliver Wendell Holmes said, "When in doubt, do it."

I'm going to share with you a simple, but profound system a colleague taught me when I was wrestling with a tough decision.

He suggested that I ask myself:

1. What is my head telling me to do?
2. What is my heart telling me to do?
3. What is my gut telling me to do?

These questions help you achieve alignment between logic (your head), emotion (your heart), and intuition (your gut).

Most of us favor one domain over the others. Some put their trust in facts and data, relying on logic to point the way. Others trust their feelings to inform their point of view. Still others rely on their hunches, developing what they might call their sixth sense. Doubt comes, in my opinion, when one relies more heavily on one domain than the others – because the others aren't being acknowledged.

I remember a time of great indecision on my part from my days at summer camp as a teenager. We were being taught how to dive from the ten meter platform – and there I was, standing on that tiny island in the sky, vacillating between launching myself into space or climbing back down the ladder in defeat.

My head told me to dive. The odds were good I would survive regardless of my skill. How many kids, I asked myself, have ever died or ended up paraplegics from a high dive? None that I knew of.

My heart screamed "Abort! Abort!" I was crippled with fear. I could not move.

My gut was cautiously optimistic. My instincts were telling me that I would be fine – that the coach was there to help – that this was an opportunity to stare down fear's throat and laugh.

I stood there for several moments (which seemed like hours). I was wracked with doubt. My head, heart and gut were out of alignment. But I was a young grasshopper, and had not yet learned the ways of the Three Questions.

Finally, my fear of humiliation which would result from quitting was overwhelmed by my need for inclusion with my friends, all of whom had completed a successful dive.

I launched my body into the air…

And did a ten-meter belly flop, knocking the air out of my lungs, and sending me to the bottom of the pool, where I had blacked out momentarily until the lifeguard pulled me out and gave me mouth-to-mouth resuscitation.

Today I recognize that my high diving decision was not a Four Percenter. I could have simply followed the advice of Oliver Wendell Holmes, who said, "When in doubt, just do it."

When the stakes are high, when the probability is good that this decision is a Four Percenter, it makes good sense to tune in and listen to what your head, heart and gut are saying, rather than discounting them. Clues to your doubts can be found in the domains you try to ignore.

Ask yourself – if my head, heart and gut aren't aligned, what needs to be reconsidered to get them to "fly in formation"? Perhaps there is a better decision to be made, which can alleviate your doubt.

Then again, perhaps you won't remove all doubt. If you've reached a decision, listened to your head, heart and gut, and still have some doubts, act anyway. The odds are it won't really matter in the end what you decide. If it *does* turn out to be a Four Percenter, you can take comfort in the words of the writer Marilyn Moats Kennedy, who said, "It's better to be boldly decisive and risk being wrong than to agonize at length and be right too late."

Just do it.

CHAPTER SEVENTEEN

Burying Dead Horses

How many meetings have you attended which drag on and on, as people "beat a dead horse" in the search for agreement on how to resolve an issue before them?

I watched a meeting unfolding of the directors of a new company, who were trying to decide which vendor would supply a key service to the organization. After many minutes of heated debate, the frustrated Director of Business Development, who chaired the meeting, literally stood up and pounded his fist on the table.

That got everyone's attention!

"I believe strongly we should use Consolidated Products! Does anyone have a problem with that?"

The room fell silent.

"Anyone?"

More silence.

At last he said (and this is the best part), "I guess we have consensus. Let's move on!"

Did they have consensus?

Nope.

They had silence. They had intimidation, fear, and probably a fair share of resentment. But they did not have consensus.

WHAT IS CONSENSUS?

Consensus is one of the most misunderstood concepts in organizations today. Because it can be confusing, meetings can drag on forever. So what is it? Consensus is an agreement with two critical characteristics:

1. Everyone in the room agrees they can live with it, and

2. They further agree to support it should it be adopted.

Consensus is achieved when each person has decided that a particular option, while perhaps not being exactly what they would have chosen, is "close enough." Furthermore, everyone is willing to support the decision as though it was the one they would have chosen. They agree not to sabotage it, second-guess it, or take no responsibility for it.

WHAT CONSENSUS IS NOT

- It's not unanimity, with everyone in 100% agreement with a proposal
- It's not majority rule
- It's not silence
- It's not horse trading ("I'll support you on this one, if you'll support me on that one.")

· It's certainly not something you have achieved
  simply because time is running out leading
  everyone to throw in the towel

How do you reach consensus with a group, a decision-making style called the *Life Raft* (see Chapter 15)? You must set a climate where people are willing to do two things:

1. **Plant their stake.** They must be willing to let
   people know where they stand and how they feel.
   Planting your stake means putting options on the
   table (if only to make sure they're considered). It
   means to participate.

2. **Move their stake.** After hearing from others,
   people need to be willing to be influenced and
   change their position. Their goal is to find the
   best thinking of the group, rather than bolstering
   arguments on their own position. They must seek
   to understand other positions, not to prevail in
   the discussion.

You will never have consensus if people refuse to plant their stake, or if people aren't willing to move their stake. How do you get them to do that?

There are three things you must do, as the meeting leader, to help your team achieve consensus:

1. Set the stage.
2. Facilitate the process.
3. Check for consensus.

SET THE STAGE

Consensus rarely emerges naturally, unless all already were close in agreement.

If you want consensus, you must prepare the group before the discussion. Begin by reminding them what consensus is (and isn't), and then lay some ground rules:

- Everyone in the group has an equal stake in finding the best solution.

- Everyone is expected to participate – to offer proposals, to share their reasoning, to clarify their positions

- Everyone is also expected to remain open to moving their stake, to be influenced.

- Last, and definitely not least, everyone agrees beforehand that once the group achieves consensus, they will actively support the decision.

FACILITATE THE PROCESS

Once you've set the ground rules, the group can engage in finding an acceptable solution or decision. As the dialogue begins, pay attention to the following:

- Make sure everyone is participating. If necessary, ask people directly where their stake is at the moment.

- To improve the quality of the decision, play "devil's advocate" from time to time, putting alternatives on the table that have not been discussed and may not be anyone's "stake."

· Ask people to take the rest of the team through their thought-process. For example, suppose sales of an important product are down. As the discussion unfolds, someone makes the following proposal: "We need to hire some new engineers." In order for the group to understand this stake, ask them:

» What data did you start with? *Sales of that product are down 12% from last year.*

» What meaning do you attach to that data? *Our products are becoming inferior to those of our competitors.*

» What assumptions are you making based on the meaning you've attached? *Our engineers are relying on outmoded technology.*

» What conclusions are you drawing? *Our engineers are holding us back. They aren't staying current in the technology.*

» What beliefs are you adopting from those conclusions? *We can't count on our current engineers.*

» What action are you proposing? *We must hire some new, smart, talented engineers who are able to employ the latest technology.*

· Make good use of white boards or flip charts so people can see all the proposals at the same time.

· If there are lots of ideas, consider "multivoting" to pare down the list:

» Give everyone about three red dot stickies for every ten ideas to be considered.

> » Have them "vote" by placing the dots on the proposals they feel are the most useful. They can place all their dots on one proposal, or spread them around as they see fit.
>
> » Total the number of dots on each suggestion. You will probably find half or more of the list falls well short of the others. These proposals can be eliminated.

CHECKING FOR CONSENSUS

As the discussion moves along, you may begin to wonder how close you are to reaching consensus. Fortunately, there's a simple test that's deceptively easy and nearly fool-proof.

If the discussion has begun to drag, and you sense that the horse has probably met his maker, you can check for consensus by asking everyone for a show of thumbs.

A show of thumbs?

Exactly.

People can put their thumbs up to mean "I agree with this proposal completely."

Thumbs down means "I can't support this proposal yet."

But most important, people can point their thumb to the side (parallel to the ground) to mean, "Although this is not exactly what I would propose we can do, I can live with it and agree to support it."

Consensus is defined, behaviorally, as a decision which passes the thumb test – every thumb is either pointed up or to the side. If there's a thumb or two pointed down, the horse is still breathing, and the dialogue must be allowed to continue. But if there are no thumbs down, you are finished. You have reached consensus. You do not need to convince those with sideways thumbs to turn them up.

Once you've achieved consensus, remember to refresh the group's memory of what it means – you have reached a decision that each member of the team can live with, and that all have agreed to support.

In a way, it's pretty simple – when you get your team to plant their stakes while being willing to move them.

CHAPTER EIGHTEEN

Please Go On Meeting This Way!

Humorist Ashleigh Brilliant said, "Our meetings are held to discuss many problems which would never arise if we held fewer meetings.

Popular radio host Fred Allen, of the 1930s and 1940s, believed that "A meeting is a gathering of people who singly can do nothing, but together can decide that nothing can be done."

Almost everyone has a distaste for meetings – especially staff meetings which take on a life of their own. Complaints about business meetings are legion:

- They aren't well planned
- They are poorly facilitated
- They go off-track
- The decision-making process is unclear
- The right people aren't there
- The wrong people are there
- There's no agenda
- Nothing gets resolved
- There's little or no follow-up between meetings
- There are too many side conversations
- They don't start on time

- The don't end on time
- They happen too frequently
- Some people talk too much
- Some people don't talk enough

As one cynic said, "A meeting is an event where minutes are taken and hours wasted."

Now that you're a manager, you're not only going to have to attend meetings, you're going to be expected to run them – particularly staff meetings. Oh, no!

Don't panic — there's good news. You can learn to run staff meetings which are more productive, consume less time, feature useful participation, produce higher quality decisions and lead to better performance results.

It's not rocket science. All it takes is some planning up front, a few simple tools and techniques which really work, and your willingness to use these tools. Here are some suggestions:

PLAN YOUR MEETINGS

Begin by deciding a clear *purpose* for the meeting.

Every meeting – even a weekly staff meeting – should have a purpose beyond "It's Tuesday morning." A clear purpose to have a meeting might be:

- To create a plan
- To set goals
- To make a decision
- To measure progress

- To provide feedback
- To share information
- To solve a problem

You know your purpose is clear if you can easily picture an outcome that would tell you when the meeting is over:

- The plan is drafted
- The goals are established
- The decision is made
- Everyone is aware of the status of a project
- Etc.

USE AN AGENDA

An agenda is perhaps the most important tool for any meeting, which makes it astonishing to see how often it's forgotten. An agenda should:

- State the purpose and intended outcome of the meeting
- List the topics to be discussed, in order of priority
- Set preliminary time limits for each topic (subject to negotiation at the meeting)
- Label each item "info exchange" or "decision needed" to further clarify the expectations

Create a process for your staff to add items to the staff meeting agenda a few days before each meeting, and publish by email the agenda to everyone the day before. That said, do not create an expectation that everyone on your staff should have an item for the agenda at each meeting, or that they should have a status update every time.

FACILITATE THE MEETING

1. Start each meeting with a brief check-in process.

   This gives people the opportunity to make the mental transition from what's happening outside the meeting to what's happening at the meeting.

2. Establish good ground rules and remind people of them. Some of my favorites include:

   · Be here, now.

   · Start on time, end on time.

   · We are all 100% responsible for the effectiveness of the meeting.

   · Be willing to plant your stake, and be willing to move it. (In other words, be willing to share your opinion or position on an issue, and be willing to be influenced by others.)

3. Involve your staff in different meeting roles.

   · Have someone record the agreements as they are made.

   · Have someone serve as time-keeper to (gently) remind the group of how much time is available or has been used for any given topic.

   · Have different people serve as the facilitator for the meeting. This person's role is to keep the group focused, guide the flow of the discussion, remain neutral

on the issues, and look for ways to
improve the process of the meeting.

DEAL WITH PROBLEMS

During the meeting there are four kinds of "participation problems" which often come up: side conversations, participants who don't talk enough, participants who talk too much, and participants who are confrontational.

SIDE CONVERSATIONS TECHNIQUES:

- Simply make a public observation: "We have side conversations going on."
- Ask if someone in the sidebar has something to share with the larger group
- Ask if the conversation can be taken off-line

WHEN PEOPLE AREN'T SPEAKING UP:

- Ask them direct, open-ended questions (which can't be answered yes/no or with a single word or two)
- Consider breaking the group into smaller groups or even pairs or trios, who could report back to the larger group their input on an issue
- Occasionally poll the entire group one by one on an issue
- Coach the reluctant participants off-line

WHEN PEOPLE ARE TALKING TOO MUCH:

- When they pause for air, say "In the interest of time…" and offer a summary of their input.

- Literally interrupt them by saying, "Let me piggyback on that comment…" and add your own input

- Deflect to another participant, by saying, "Interesting, Jim. I'd like to get Ann's perspective as well."

IF PEOPLE ARE CONFRONTATIONAL, TRY THIS:

- Paraphrase their comment without the "hot button" language (Change "Those idiots in HR are jamming this down our throats!" to "The concern is whether HR is aware of the impact of these policy changes on our department.")

- Agree with any neutral aspect of the comment that you can, and move on

- Make a neutral observation: "This seems to be an issue which raises a lot of passion."

As the meeting unfolds, there are several other tips that will be useful:

- Use a "parking lot" to keep people on track. Take a piece of flip chart paper and label it the Parking Lot. When people have a thought about something that's not on topic but worth bringing up, have them offer the thought and capture it on the Parking Lot. Then get back to the issue at hand. Before the meeting ends, return to the Parking Lot and see what issues shown there have been resolved, need discussion today, or should be assigned to someone for action before the next meeting.

- Be conscious of the meeting environment, including factors such as taking breaks, serving food, etc.

- Make "I-statements" when you want to bring the group's attention to it's process.

  - "Maybe it's only me, but I seem to have lost that last point."

  - "I'm wondering if we've drifted off topic."

EVALUATE THE MEETING

A good habit is to evaluate your meetings periodically to see how they might be improved.

One tool is a simple 3x5 index card. Give one to each participant, and ask them: on a scale of 1-10 (one is lousy, ten is fantastic), how well did this meeting go?

After everyone has written down their number, ask, "What is one suggestion you could make that could move us up a notch? For example, if you wrote down a six, what would have to happen for you to change the rating to a seven next time?" Do not ask for any names on the cards.

Collect the cards, read the suggestions after the meting, and report back to the group at the next meeting what you've learned. In this way, the group can take ownership of the meetings, the ground rules, and the agreements they've made with each other.

Last, but not least. Add a little variety to your meetings. Hold one at a coffee house, another on a walk outdoors. Have everyone stand for the entire meeting – this will definitely help keep it short!

You can run good meetings

Meetings are effective when they have *structure*. They are successful when you pay attention to the *process* as much as the task. They are *productive* when people understand their role, the ground rules, and the expectations about the purpose and outcome of the meeting.

Part Five: Three More Things

The last three Quick Start chapters just didn't fit anywhere else. They will show you how to be a "fly on the wall" to learn what others are saying about your management practice (and how you can improve it), present some ideas about how to manage your boss, and summarize the best advice I can offer you – on how to respond to requests for advice.

CHAPTER NINETEEN

How to Be a Fly on the Wall

I've yet to meet the manager who wouldn't like to be a fly on the wall, able to hear what others are saying about his or her performance as a leader. It's hard to know what others think and feel. Even your performance review doesn't capture it, because the person who does your review is the person who knows the least about what it's like to work for you.

To help managers understand their impact on others, organizations spend big bucks on something called a "360 degree feedback" process. This is a questionnaire, completed by you, your boss, your peers and your staff that focuses on a list of management competencies. The numbers are crunched and any comments are recorded (anonymously). You get a report which compares your perceptions with those of other people.

From there, you can create a plan to develop skills in those areas that might need improvement. It's a fantastic process with one major flaw – it can be expensive. Fortunately, you can replicate the results for free.

You'll need the help of an independent, objective, and trusted colleague. You might find someone in Human Resources, or even someone outside your organization to help for free (perhaps by offering to return the favor). You'll ask this person to do three things:

1. Collect some information from your boss, your peers and your staff about you.

2. Hold that information in confidence in terms of revealing who said what about you.

3. Share the aggregate information (without attribution) with you.

You don't even need a list of management competencies to get useful information. Just take a piece of paper, and write down either of these sets of three questions:

1. What should I start doing, or do more often?

2. What should I stop doing, or do less often?

3. What should I continue to do?

1. What am I doing well?

2. What am I doing not so well?

3. What suggestions do you have for my professional development?

How to work the process

1. Hold a meeting to explain this process and introduce the colleague who will be gathering the data.

    »   Make sure everyone understands that the process is both voluntary and confidential

    »   Give them the questionnaire and a stamped envelope addressed to your colleague.

» Make sure there's a reasonable deadline.

2. Have the colleague collect the information and assemble it for you in a way that protects the anonymity of those who choose to participate (for instance, retyping the responses and putting them in alphabetical order).

3. Read the collected results carefully (perhaps with the help of the colleague).

   » Seek to understand what's being said.

   » Do not seek to determine who said what.

   » Determine what you'll do with the information.

   » What behaviors are you going to address?

   » What plan will you set in place for further professional development?

   » What feedback did you receive that you do not plan to address in the near future?

4. Hold another meeting (or a series of meetings) to:

   » Share what you've learned about yourself.

   » Seek clarification about anything that's confused you (but again, without trying to determine who said what. You ask questions like, "Why might someone believe I'm not spending enough time in the field?" so that anyone can share an idea, not just the person who wrote the comment.)

» Thank them for their participation – even if not all of the invited participants chose to do so.

You can be a fly on the wall from time to time. This method is virtually free, and it can reveal much. Knowledge about your team's perception of you is critical to becoming the best manager you can be.

CHAPTER TWENTY

Don't Forget to Manage Your Boss

The *hardest* person you're going to have to learn to manage is yourself. If you're like me, that's a lifelong process.

The *most important* person you're going to have manage is your boss.

Your boss is critical to your success. Peter Drucker, in his book *The Practice of Management*, says "You don't have to like or admire your boss, nor do you have to hate him. You do have to manage him, however, so that he becomes your resource for achievement, accomplishment, and personal success."

Managing your boss is not the same as managing your staff. Let's face it – you can't fire your boss, nor can you discipline the boss for poor performance. You can't rely at all on your positional power to get results.

But if you can learn to manage "up," you can manage in any direction. You can apply the principles to managing your peers, your clients, and even your customers. In fact, you're already doing this on some level, but without being aware of how to manage your boss, and without a plan, you may not be doing it very well. Let's bring it to consciousness and make it work for you.

Managing your boss doesn't mean manipulating your boss; it's not about tricking your boss into doing things he or she wouldn't otherwise do. It's about building a strong, win-win relationship with the person who will have a major impact on your career. The responsibility for building that relationship is yours. 100%. After all, it's your own self-interest that's at stake here.

There are many resources on the internet with tips on how to manage your boss. Let's focus on three things which are paramount:

1. You must find ways to inspire your boss's confidence in your competence.

2. You must learn your boss's management, communication, and interpersonal styles and adapt your behavior to work well with them.

3. You must learn your boss's fundamental expectations and then deliver the goods.

One more that gets scant attention: *learn your boss's pet peeves and respect them.* If your boss isn't a morning person – time your visits for the afternoon. If your boss hates email, deliver your status updates in person (and send a simple follow-up email afterwards). If your boss hates chit-chat, make sure you come straight to the point when you talk.

Think of it this way – if you manage *your boss* well, your boss can manage *you* well.

CHAPTER TWENTY ONE

The Best Advice I Can Give You

One of the surprising things about becoming a manager to many people is how often you are asked for advice, particularly from their new staff. You may be caught off-guard at all this attention.

Let me give you a piece of advice: *never give anyone a piece of advice.*

Charles Varlet La Grange, a French actor in the 17th century got it right when he said, "When we ask advice we are usually looking for an accomplice."

"No one wants advice - only corroboration," echoed John Steinbeck.

It's bad business for managers to get into the advice-giving business.

It starts innocently enough. You'll get all kinds of questions:

· Should I take the promotion?

· Should I go back to school?

· How should I handle my problem with my co-worker?

You get the idea.

People will be coming to you because you're now seen as an authority figure. You're a *manager*. You must *know* stuff. In many cases, you actually *do* know stuff. You've had experience managing your own career. You may know a lot about the organization. You might have a good idea about how your employee should handle that problem with her co-worker.

But let me say it again:

> *Never give anyone*
> *a piece of advice,*
> *even when they ask for it.*

After all, as Erica Jong puts it, "Advice is what we ask for when we already know the answer but wish we didn't."

Many managers (and others) love to give advice. It gives us the warm glow of feeling wise, and being helpful to someone in need. We feel important and our accomplishments in life are being validated. Who doesn't want to be sought-after and possibly make a difference in someone's life?

It's a trap. If you offer advice and it's accepted but fails to work out, the advice seeker will blame you for the result. If you offer advice and it's ignored, you'll be left wondering why your advice was requested in the first place.

Help the seeker explore options

Rather than saying things like:

· Here's what I'd do…

- That's easy. You should…
- Ah yes, I've been through this myself. Here's what I did (and, by implication, you should do)…

Says things like this:
- What are your choices?
- Have you considered this? Or this? Or that?
- What do you think would happen if you chose that particular option?
- What are the upsides of this possibility?
- What are the downsides?
- What's your head telling you to do?
- What's your heart telling you to do?
- What's your gut telling you to do?
- Are you aware of these resources that are available to you? (For instance, the company's tuition reimbursement policy or the employee assistance program.)

HERE'S WHAT YOU CAN DO

Stay neutral.

Help them think it through on their own.

Suggest resources they may not know exist.

Make your life as a manager a little bit easier, by not offering advice to anyone – whether they ask for it or not.

Novelist Edgar Watson Howe put it this way: "A good scare is worth more to a man than good advice." People grow when they have to puzzle things out for themselves, and the best advice will always be what emerges from within. Help them find their own "path with heart" and set aside your own need to feel wise.

On the subject of giving advice, that's the best advice I can give you.

Creating A Professional Development Plan

Perhaps the most important commitment you can make is to create and implement an on-going Professional Development Plan which may unfold throughout your career. There's always going to be something to learn.

There are at least three people you may want to help you craft your plan – your boss, your mentor (if you have one) and someone from Human Resources (because they usually are up-to-speed with learning opportunities such as educational programs, seminars and workshops, and the like).

What I'd suggest is that when you put together your plan, consider all of the following elements. Some will be more important to you than others at different times in your career. All have potential value.

- **Self development** – things like books, audio and video tapes, self-guided workbooks, computer-based training, webinars, and the like.

- **Formal educational programs** at accredited universities. While an advanced degree might be helpful, don't forget many universities offer certificate programs in specialized areas of interest.

- **Mentoring and coaching relationships** with people you admire.

- **Internal training programs** – Many organizations have top-grade management development programs for managers, who also enjoy the benefit of rubbing elbows with other managers they might otherwise not meet.

- **External training programs** – The good ones provide an excellent opportunity to learn new skills *and* explore new ideas offered by both the facilitators and other participants from other organizations.

- **Job rotation** – Sometimes, the best development plan is to take yourself out of your comfort zone by managing a different function for a year or two.

- **Special assignments** – Leading a cross-functional project team can provide an opportunity to stretch your management skills.

- **Time on the present job** with a specific focus on a specific skill is critical. Work with your mentor and/or boss to identify areas for improvement and hold yourself accountable for getting results.

"Owners Manuals" I Highly Recommend

I hope you've enjoyed your Quick Start guide to becoming an effective manager. You've been given ideas that are important to think about during your transition. It's been my goal to get you "up and running" with confidence, purpose and direction.

Just as my digital camera came with both a Quick Start guide *and* an Owner's Manual, which explained all of the features of the camera in great detail, successful managers can explore all of the ideas in this book - and many more, in much more depth. I call these books "Owner's Manuals" for managers.

It can be a bit bewildering to know where to start. As I wrote this, there were over 600,000 books listed on amazon.com with the search word "management." There are over 62,000 just on "leadership."

So where do you go from here?

Allow me to offer my personal Top Ten list of "Owner's Manuals" for managers that have served me and my clients well over the years. You could start with any of these and begin to expand your understanding of leadership and management.

1. *A Whack on the Side of the Head: How You Can Be More Creative*, by Roger Von Oech, 2008.

This isn't a "management" or "leadership" book per se – it's a wonderful roadmap to becoming more creative. Since leadership is highly connected to innovation, this book could be an important tool for you and your team.

2. *Managing Management Time: Who's Got the Monkey*, by William Oncken, 1987.

This one's been around a while, and it's become a classic. The book began as an article in the Harvard Review, and quickly became a top ten reprint. Oncken went back to the drawing board and expanded the article into a book. Easy to read, easy to understand, and about as practical a guide to good management as I've come across. His piece on the "Levels of Initiative" is not to be missed.

3. *Managing Transitions: Making the Most of Change*, by William Bridges, 2009.

Bridges was the first, to my knowledge, to make a practical distinction between "change" and "transition." Change happens *to* us, and transition happens *inside* us. You don't just manage change in an organization, you must pay attention to the stages of transition if you want your change effort to succeed. Strongly recommended.

4. *On Becoming a Leader*, by Warren Bennis, 2009.

Bennis is one of the best at sorting out the differences between management and leadership, and has emerged as a seminal thinker on the subject. Actually, I'd recommend almost any book by Bennis as being critical to your development in a management career.

5. *Switch: How to Change Things, When Change is Hard*, by Chip Heath and Dan Heath, 2010.

The Heath brothers have just published an enjoyable, easy-to-read book on managing change. Filled with stunning and insightful true stories, you'll find practical ideas on how to shepherd your next change effort. Well worth your time.

6. *The Fifth Discipline: The Art & Practice of the Learning Organization*, by Peter Senge, 2006.

Warning: this book is massive and deep. I'd put this on my reading list, but I wouldn't start here. That said, this is a go-to book to understand power and politics in organizations.

7. *The Leadership Challenge*, by James M. Kouzes and Barry Z. Posner, 2008.

Kouzes and Posner have organized the practices of effective managers into five elements, and they've done it in a way that's quite reader-friendly. This is the book I'd probably recommend first after reading the Quick Start Guide. It will provide you with lots of great ideas on management habits you'll want to develop.

8. *The Path of Least Resistance for Managers*, by Robert Fritz and Peter Senge, 1999.

If you'd like a fundamental understanding of why people do what they do (and perhaps not what you'd like them to do!) this is your book. You'll understand the psychology and the importance of the concept of vision and its role in motivating yourself and others.

9. *To Do or Not To Do: How Successful Leaders Make Better Decisions*, by Gary Winters and Eric Klein, 2004.

I can't pass the opportunity to make an unabashed plug for my other book. For a full explanation of the principles behind effective decision making - especially in terms of how and when to involve your team in your decisions, this will give you simple and practical tools and techniques.

10. *Up the Organization: How to Stop the Corporation from Stifling People and Strangling Profits*, by Robert Townsend, republished in 2007.

This is an odd book to recommend to new and emerging managers, but I'm putting it on the list anyway. Townsend was the CEO of Avis Rent-A-Car back when they ran the popular and hugely successful "We try harder," campaign, and he put together his own leadership manifesto that's unique in the literature. He has strong, common-sense principles that may seem directed at other senior managers, but they can be translated into things *every* manager can adapt. It's a profoundly simple book with timeless wisdom. Buy it. Read it. Enjoy it.

Made in the USA
San Bernardino, CA
17 September 2016